NICE GUYS FINISH *first*

BARRIE BERGMAN

**Treat the Universe
in an ethical manner
and the Universe
will take care of you.**
Buckminster Fuller

**It's only rock n' roll
but I like it**
Rolling Stones

For Arlene

Table of Contents

Prologue

It's Only Rock 'n' Roll, But I Like It
From Music Fan to Rockin' CEO

You might be wondering, "Who is Barrie Bergman and why should I care about what he has to say?" I have built successful multi-million-dollar businesses and my purpose here is to share my experiences with you.

In our society, and particularly in business, we are creating a huge group of jerks. We expect boorish unethical behavior from business people. This behavior is unacceptable. It will not win. These people will not get rich and be happy. They will be miserable S.O.B.s. I'm convinced that you can be a good person and do well in business and in your personal life. There are enough idiots out there. The world needs more ethical people. Whoever said that nice guys finish last was just another jerk trying to justify his existence.

Over the years, I've been able to observe what works and what doesn't work in business. I found that it takes great character strength to keep your integrity intact when the pressure is on. Adhering to strong ethical principles is key to my philosophy for success, along with treating people with kindness and respect, and having fun while you strive to make things happen. I think it's important to be able to sleep at night, feeling satisfied not only with your work, but with how you conduct yourself as a person in the process.

My first experience with growing a successful business, and the one I hold closest to my heart, was building a company called Record Bar from a mom & pop enterprise in North Carolina to the second largest record store chain in the United States. I'm a music lover and Record Bar's growth was fueled in part by my personal passion—that, and the efforts of many talented, dedicated people.

People always came first, my customers, my employees, and my relationship with my wife, Arlene. We wanted the stores to be a great environment to hang out in for the consumer. We accomplished this by creating a happy atmosphere for the consumers and the employees. As we grew we kept the same formula for multiple stores, an office, and warehouse. Happy people create a good feeling environment.

We created a culture that honored, developed, and rewarded our people. Record Bar was known throughout the industry for being an innovative and forward thinking company, for having the very best people, and for being a fun and stimulating place to work. At Record Bar, it always felt like we were family, even after we grew to nearly 2,000 employees. Our people were deeply loyal. Everyone worked very hard and we all had a great time in the process.

We weren't always conventional. Record Bar was one of the first corporations to provide employees a motivational weekend experience that included the now famous Firewalk. This was in the early 80's, and our pioneering efforts generated a great deal of controversy. I took a lot of public relations flak for that one, but the majority of our people were empowered by it. We were just ahead of our time.

For many years Record Bar enjoyed a continuous rise in revenues, growing at a sustained rate of 20-30% a year. But things weren't always rosy. In 1984, the company took a nearly fatal nosedive, raking in losses of $5-6 million over a two-year period. It wasn't easy, but we regained our upward trajectory. I learned an awful lot about what not to do and how to right wrongs during that chapter in our history. In 1989, Record Bar sold for $92 million, and I retired in comfort at the ripe old age of 47.

I got bored very quickly with early retirement, and started looking for something else to do. I joined forces with a partner, John Hansen, and we bailed out a failing natural cosmetics company based in California. Together with Leslie Blodgett, we took Bare Escentuals from the verge of bankruptcy to a burgeoning international enterprise. In 2004, fourteen years after we took the helm, Bare Escentuals sold for over $200 million. I found that the strategies, theories and philosophies I had developed at Record Bar were indeed universally applicable to growing a business in any industry.

My business success is only part of the story. I've also been happily married to the same woman for over 45 years. I believe wholeheartedly that people who are successful, are successful. That means if you are going to be successful in business, it is important to give attention and commitment to being successful in your personal life as well. Striking a healthy balance is vitally important. If your personal life isn't working, your business endeavors aren't going to work that well either. All work and no play makes Jack a dull boy.

So, why should you read this book? If you've ever desired to succeed, to get rich, and to be a good person with a personal life that is balanced, fulfilling, and fun, this book will show you a way to make it happen. The simple strategies below are what worked, and with these you can build a successful business and a successful life:

- Enjoy your job

- Find a balance in your life

- Treat coworkers with respect and understanding

- Set goals based on excellence not based on money

How I Became a Music Man

I often marvel at the series of events that led me down the path to becoming a millionaire in the music industry. For as long as I can remember, I've had a passion for music and for being around anyone who made music. Early on, my dream was to go to New York and work for one of the big record labels. I wanted to be a player in the music business and make things happen.

As a child, I would spend hours listening to the radio. Radio was a different animal then and a station would play all different kinds of music. They would have the Gospel Hour, the Black Music Hour, and the Country Hour. I loved it all. But when stations started playing "The Devil's Music"—Rock 'n' Roll—I was in Heaven!

In addition to radio, I had a ton of records to listen to because of a quirky turn of events in my father's life. During World War II, a man borrowed money from my father and wasn't able to pay him back in cash. Instead, he paid him off with a warehouse full of jukeboxes. My father would bring home armloads of 78's, and later 45's, and we'd all listen to the music. I started becoming a major record collector at the age of ten. In junior high, I was a big hit at the sock hops and the school dances because I was the kid with all the records.

If that wasn't enough to feed my passion for music, my uncle owned a record store in Durham, North Carolina. I was just 14 years old when I got the chance to work weekends in my uncle's store and I loved every minute of it. On my lunch breaks, I would go off by myself and read the trade magazines cover to cover. I had a bad case of hero worship for the musicians and anybody who worked with them. I was particularly in awe of the marketing VPs of the record labels, because they got to meet all of the music stars. I aspired to be one of them.

I had been working in my uncle's record store for three years when things changed dramatically for my family. My father had been making a good living in the wholesale grocery business until the big chain stores came along and ran the family-owned grocers out of business. While I was still in high school, my father went bankrupt. The only thing my father had left was the jukebox business, which by then had evolved into a fledgling record store that had never made money. He decided his best bet for generating a steady income again was to put his energy into building a profitable retail music store. It was by utter coincidence that my father and my uncle both owned record stores.

At seventeen years old, I was the only one in my immediate family who knew anything about operating a music store, so I started teaching my father. My father was very good at merchandising, i.e. he knew how to sell things, but he didn't know anything about the music business. On weekends when I was in high school and in college, I used to drive 33 miles to Burlington to work in my father's store. Together we were a fairly good team–except that we fought all the time. I just hated working for him, but I learned a lot.

Two years later, after we got the hang of running our new record store, my uncle decided to move away from Durham. He sold his store, called The Record Bar, to my mother and father. Now we had two stores. While I was in college at Duke, my father saw a promising opportunity to open a store in Chapel Hill. We had a lot of music and Chapel Hill had a lot of college kids. We couldn't afford three stores, so we closed the Burlington store and moved everything to Chapel Hill. My father asked me to leave Duke and come manage the Chapel Hill store full time. That's when my wife Arlene and I got married and opened our first store, in 1963.

Originally, when I agreed to run the store for my father, I said I didn't want to be a record store manager for the rest of my life. I was going to give it five years then go to New York to work in the heart of the music industry. Of course, after five years, when both stores were doing quite well, my father wanted me to stay.

I told my father I would reconsider my decision to go to New York under one condition. We had to expand and open more stores. That's when we started looking for store #3. We opened our third store in a shopping mall in Raleigh, which was an innovative move at the time, since record stores had not typically been located in malls. The mall concept was a winner and we began to expand quite rapidly.

My father had been content with two stores, and my mother was dead set against expansion, fearing it would lead to another bankruptcy. But my dreams were big. I thought the greatest thing in the world would be to someday have five stores. I could hardly imagine how amazing that would be. We'd own the world! When we grew to five stores, I aimed my sights at ten. This was in the '70s when there weren't many chains in the record business. I realized as we grew that I could be a player in the music business and stay right there in Chapel Hill.

After opening our 9th store, my father opted out and let me run the company. One day we had a staff meeting and my father announced, "Today I'm making Barrie the President." He not only said it, but he acted like it, also. He came in every day for the next 15 years and read the newspaper, giving me free rein to run the business. In the history of fathers and sons in business together, that's pretty unique. Usually one of them gets carried out feet first. But that didn't happen. He stayed out of my way and let me run the business.

Having a Rockin' Good Time

Most existing music stores were small mom and pop operations. They had tiny inventories, and the employees weren't very friendly. We put in extensive inventories with a large variety of music and trained our employees to be friendly and courteous to every customer, no matter what their musical taste. We worked to establish Record Bar as a brand that stood for excellence in customer service, where a customer would feel welcome and could enjoy browsing in our stores. After all, music is all about being joyful.

Ultimately, Record Bar grew to a nationwide chain of over 200 stores. We gained a position in the music industry where our percentage of sales made a difference, and my opinion mattered. I became President of the industry association, NARM, the National Association of Recording Merchandisers. In 1980 I was named in *Rolling Stone* as one of the Heavy Hundred influential people in the industry. I had become an important player and when I talked, people listened. Not only could I meet the music stars I wanted to know, the record labels were clamoring to have them meet me!

This was in the golden days when record companies were thriving. They pulled out all the stops to wine and dine the influential people in the industry. They gave away exotic trips, threw lavish parties with incredible music and provided unbelievable gifts. They also sent me a lot of music, and being the collector that I am, it was bliss. I got to have whatever I wanted, sometimes as many as 50 albums a week. I acquired some magnificent collector's items, including the original Elvis Presley albums and the original Buddy Holly album.

By far, the biggest perk was meeting the people. I was star-struck from the get-go and I still am. A wall in my office is filled with memorabilia and photos of my wife and me with such celebrities as Bruce Springsteen, Michael Jackson, Lyle Lovett, Barbra Streisand, George Harrison and Stevie Nicks. I've amused my friends with anecdotes of encounters with the stars of rock and roll. For a fun diversion, I'll take you behind the scenes to glimpse some of the juicier moments.

Today in the Business World

These days, I advise organizations that get it – whose leaders understand that you can grow the business without a lot of dead bodies. I've learned a few things about success in business and life, and that's what I want to share with you in this book.

I expect that what I have to say will piss off some people. If it doesn't, I'll be disappointed. I want this book to generate conversation and thought. It won't be for everybody. Some of my ideas are controversial and I don't expect everyone to agree with me. What I can say without reservation is that these are strategies that work. It's not just some woo-woo new age attitude about the world. It's a business strategy. It worked for me, and I believe it can work for you. So take my advice or not--it's up to you--but I hope it's an enjoyable thought-provoking read.

Part I:

Money Changes Everything

Chapter 1

We'll Get Rich A Few Days Later
Adhering to ethics

I've had the good fortune to experience financial success in business. I've been instrumental in growing two great companies that started out as fledgling start-ups and became industry giants. I have also dabbled in various and sundry other business ventures. In all my business dealings, I've done my best to treat people the way I wanted to be treated in return. It's a very effective style, it made me a lot of money and I always felt good while I was doing it.

I'm an amoral person. I don't blindly subscribe to what the culture dictates. To me, morals are a set of arbitrary norms made up by society and vary from culture to culture, religion to religion. Ethics, on the other hand, are universal truths. I'm a very ethical person. In fact, I'm absolutely evangelical about ethics.

To me, being ethical is fairly simple. It means adhering to an unyielding standard of honesty and integrity in all business and personal dealings. No matter how great the temptation for financial gain or personal power, you take the high road. You make the choice to live your life with honesty and integrity. You may get rich a few days later, but you'll be able to live your life with a clear conscience.

In business it's about being loyal to the organization that you work for and creating an organization that is loyal to the people who work there. In your personal life it's about loving and supporting your family and friends. One area is not exclusive of the other. The right to live a balanced life should be an unalienable right. It's up there with freedom of speech and going drinking on a Saturday night.

The Type-A personality and the drive to succeed at whatever the cost, has gotten us to this culture of cutthroat, doctor-the-books and free-for-all antics. It's what has gotten the folks at Enron and other high-profile business executives in trouble.

Nice guys adhere to ethical standards and nice guys do indeed finish first. I'm no saint, but life is too short to screw around with people, or to mess around with the IRS. Nothing is worth taking a chance of going to the slammer. I have nothing against guys named Bubba. I just don't want one for a roommate.

In business it's easy to cut corners. It is a slippery slope. After you cut the first small corner, the next corner is much easier to cut. Once you start small alterations in next quarter's profitability--for stock market reasons, or bank reasons, or IRS reasons--it's much easier to do it the next time in slightly larger amounts. Pretty soon it becomes standard operating procedure. In a company like Enron, they found themselves manipulating energy in entire regions of the country to the detriment of the people who lived in those areas. My philosophy has always been to just do it honestly and ethically the first time around and keep doing it that way.

When I was the guy at the top, I often used to say, "We'll get rich a few days later." If it didn't meet an ethical standard, a legal standard, and a loving standard, I didn't want to do it. Thus, we would get rich a few days later. To many people in business, this sounds like a fanciful way of doing business. It worked for me, I was successful and I did get rich.

You can be a good guy and still be successful. It works. I know that the better I treated people, the more successful I was personally. I'm not telling people to go love their neighbor just because it's the right thing to do. It is right, but it also works.

I enjoy mentoring up-and-coming CEOs. It amazes me how many times I'll hear them lament, "Barrie, is it really possible these days to be honest and ethical in business?" They will actually tell me they have gotten a lot of advice that it's just not possible, that they have to cut corners or they just won't make it. This appalls me. My answer to them is an emphatic "Yes!" Yes, you can be ethical and honest in business. Not only can you do it, but it's proven to be a very successful business model.

I wouldn't do it any other way. If I couldn't do it that way, I just wouldn't be in business. Life is too short and I want to be able to sleep at night.

Chapter 2

What Goes Around Comes Around
Getting back what you put out

I believe that something like Karma exists. I don't know why it exists and I don't know how it works. What I can tell you from personal observation is that what goes around comes around. Given a long enough period of time, good things seem to happen for people who put good in the universe. The universe just seems to take care of you. The converse is true as well. If you put crap out in the world, you get crap back. Maybe not right away, but in time, I guarantee you, it will come back to haunt you.

I don't want to get too New Agey here. When I say I believe in something like Karma, I don't mean to say I think I was Ben Franklin in a past life. Have you noticed how everyone who's had a past life reading seems to learn they've been Cleopatra or Napoleon? That's just stupid. I'd say most of us probably weren't any more famous or important in past lives than we are in this lifetime. What I do believe is that you create your own reality. Live a good life and chances are good things will come your way.

This is not to say you'll win a huge lottery prize if you've been good. Good comes around in the everyday joys of life. It doesn't have a hell of a lot to do with driving a Ferrari. Granted, driving a Ferrari is a cool experience, but it doesn't measure up to hugging your grandbaby. The simple things in life and nature are more meaningful to me.

I've noticed that people who treat other people badly tend to be miserable people in one way or another—perhaps they have health issues, relationship issues, money problems, you name it. You get back what you put out.

Take Leona Helmsley, please! She routinely treated her people like crap. Then one day, one of her people turned her in to the IRS for buying a stereo system and charging it to the business. She went to jail for a year for misappropriating a stereo. It's ludicrous—the smallness of the stereo vs. the largeness of her holdings. It's just as important to be ethical and honest in the little dealings as in the big ones. How you handle the little decisions reveals your character.

You can't treat people like crap at any level of your organization. They will eventually find a way to get you. That's the Martha Stewart story as well. Why do they do it? I don't get it. People are your greatest asset. Destroy your people and you destroy yourself.

Many people in a position of power tend to treat people who are in a subservient position very badly. I say give these people as much love and respect as anybody else. A guy I know was giving his tennis instructor a verbal lashing for being two minutes late for his lesson. Next lesson, the tennis pro ran him all over the court until he begged for mercy! What goes around comes around. And I'm here to tell you, never, ever abuse a waiter—unless you like the idea of having him spit in your food…or worse!

Some people aren't discerning at all about who they try to screw over. Little guys, big guys, and peers get the same treatment. I've watched with amusement when people who screw with me eventually get screwed themselves. Whether it's a week later, a month later, or years later they will get theirs. Like the time somebody called me up for a reference on a guy who had made my life miserable for the better part of ten years. He treated people like dirt. I gladly offered my honest assessment of his fitness for the job. And you say there's no God?

I figure a guy like that has to live with himself. He's got to wake up with himself every morning. It amazes me that some people think they can beat you up and still expect to be your best friend. Like the guy who tries to maliciously tap dance on my head one week and the next week calls me to ask for free concert tickets. I don't think so.

You can't spend every day of your life worrying and thinking "I've gotta be good or God's gonna crap on me." I don't believe in that kind of God anyway. It just seems to me that you can easily live lovingly, ethically, and honestly. Sometimes you pass up opportunities, but it evens out in the end.

Chapter 3

Greed is NOT Good
Screwing people over for the love of money

Are all rich people despicable? Does money really do bad things to people? I don't think money is the root of all evil, but it does tend to have a rather unpleasant impact on some people.

My experience is that as the money gets bigger and as the stakes rise, it creates great anxiety in people. The more there is, the more frightened people become and the more irrationally they act.

None of this makes any sense. It seems to me that if you start off with nothing and you make some money, it would be a very pleasant experience. However, many people who make money learn how to spend it even faster than they make it, and the more they acquire, the more they want.

The average person says, "If I ever had a million dollars, that would be enough!" The reality is that once you get the first million, you want two million or ten million, and it ain't ever enough. It's a very strange quirk.

The absolute preoccupation with money is mind-boggling. Often it takes over the lives of people who have it. Money can cloud judgment and play havoc with priorities.

The larger the deal, it seems, the more greedy people become. Intuitively, I would expect it to be the other way around because the way I see it, there is more than enough for everyone. In fact, it works just the opposite.

Money and its first cousin, greed, seem to change a lot of people. I have seen friends try to screw each other in business deals when the deals were wonderful for everybody, just because they wanted a little bit more of the pot. It is astounding, when there is plenty to go around. I don't get it.

My first encounter with this truism was when I first brought an investment company into our business at Record Bar. I needed an infusion of capital, and we were just coming out of a very difficult financial period. I found a company I really liked and made a deal. It was a wonderful deal for them and a good deal for me so we agreed on it. Before we could get the deal in place, the guy at the top of the investment company changed the deal on me.

It was over Christmas and I was with my family in Hilton Head. It was like my Christmas present from him, gift wrapped saying, "Screw you!" He did it because he had leverage over me and just because he could. It still rankles me to this day because there was no reason to put the squeeze on me—they had a great deal already. There was plenty to go around, but the guy got some kind of perverted pleasure out of getting more.

Like any of life's misadventures, there's always a lesson. Sure, when you're the one whose got the financial leverage, it's easy to take advantage of the situation and it's easy to get into the game of "Gotcha" and really leave someone bleeding on the table. I think you can make a good enough deal without drawing blood. I think there is always a place in a deal that is fair. That may seem fanciful to some, but I believe that.

I've always tried to make win-win deals. First of all, it makes me feel better. Secondly, you never know when you'll want to make another deal with the same people. I never want to leave somebody dying in the dirt after I make a deal with them. I want to leave them with some dignity and a feeling they've been dealt with fairly. I want to feel good about the deal, and I want to go back and make another deal later, if possible. I think in the long term it works better.

I don't think rich people are any better or any worse than anyone else. They just have higher profiles. The ones that are really bad stand out like sore thumbs and leave a lasting impression. Having money doesn't make you a bad person. Being unethical, dishonest, and disrespectful of other people does. Using money to ride roughshod over people is a blatant misuse of power. It's not worth compromising yourself to make money or to be rich. If you are rich, it's not worth compromising yourself to maintain it or to make more. Screw a friend in a deal over some money? Incredible! I see it all the time.

Chapter 4

License to Kill
Fighting the urge to do whatever it takes

I have a low tolerance for people who grant themselves a license to do whatever it takes to get their desired results. These people are so sure they are doing what's best for the world or for their corporate interest that they stop at nothing. It's a take no prisoners approach whether the goal is furthering humanitarian causes, meeting analysts' projections, or propagating religious beliefs. People in this mind set tackle the issues with a passion and fervor that gives them virtually a license to kill. A license, that is, to be unethical, obnoxious, and reckless. Taken to its ridiculous extreme, you have people blowing up abortion clinics to save babies. Killing to stop killing.

All too often righteousness leads to some form of abuse of other people's rights. There has to be intelligence and an idea of where you have to stop. No one should go over the line no matter how good the cause is, no matter how righteous. We all believe that our heartfelt cause is right or we wouldn't be out there trying to make a difference. But throwing bricks and beating people up to make a point? There has to be an ethical bell that goes off in peoples' heads that says, "This is wrong."

I've always been wary of true believers. True believers have a narrow sense of the big picture. They only see their side of an issue; only their way is the right way. I see very few absolute truths that have been handed down from above. There are usually gradations. I think people see different versions of the truth. Being diametrically opposed doesn't mean that one person is right and the other is wrong. Two individuals may just see things differently. Most issues aren't black and white. It seems to me that a judgment has to be tempered with a sense of responsibility and ethics it's not that hard to open your mind to another point of view, to make an effort to listen to divergent opinions.

In business, it's not necessary to "do whatever it takes" for the organization to do well. If it's not ethical and honest, forget about it! It's dangerous when people at the top feel like they've got a license to be dishonest. Here's the CEO of Enron, he knows the company is tottering, knows he can cook the books to keep it alive. Maybe he told himself, "I'm doing it for the shareholders," or "I'm doing it for my employees." People often try to justify unethical or dishonest behavior by saying they aren't doing it for themselves! It doesn't matter. If it's wrong, it's wrong. Beware of a feeling of power that comes with a license to do wrong.

At various American companies like Enron and HealthSouth, the subordinates all used the "just following orders" defense to blame the CEO for their illegal activities. I find it incredible in the case of HealthSouth Corporation that not one, not two, but four CFOs in succession got caught up in illegal money-laundering schemes at the behest of their fearless leader, CEO Richard Scrushy. All four arranged for plea bargains to testify against their boss. Every one of them said, "It's Scrushy's fault." Plea bargain or not, they could have done jail time. I don't get it. Why didn't even one of them have the balls to say,

"Screw you, I'm not going to do this." Playing follow the leader is a risky game when your leader engages in unlawful behavior.

Where does an individual draw the line when given a direct order from a superior that is at odds with what they believe to be right? Is saying no worth getting fired over? Or do they just go ahead and do something illegal, unethical or crappy to another human being? Adolf Eichmann got hanged for just following orders. Look at the ruined lives of the guards at Abu Ghraib Prison who say they were just following orders. Just following orders is not an excuse for unethical behavior.

If someone at Abu Ghraib just had the guts to speak up maybe an international crisis could have been averted. Where was that someone who should have spoken up to say, "Hey, it's not right to treat prisoners this way." I realize it's easy for me to say this from a safe distance. In a war zone, most situations are dangerous, with a real possibility you could get yourself shot. Whether in military, corporate or personal life, we face ethical conundrums everyday. It's a damn tough decision to make. However, I believe you can never go wrong taking the ethical path.

Nothing gives us the right to be unethical, dishonest or mistreat other human beings. No matter how righteous the cause, it is never a license to kill.

Chapter 5

Money Can Buy Fun Toys
But it can't buy love

I've been rich and I've been poor. Rich beats the crap out of poor. Money can be a wonderful addition to your life, if managed properly. It doesn't have to change everything; you've just got to have perspective. But I have to say, that old cliché, money can't buy happiness, is the truth.

Money's only good for the fun it will get you. I confess to having bought some really cool toys with mine. As a kid, I was as passionate about exotic cars as I was about music. The day I bought my first Ferrari was the fulfillment of a lifelong dream. Here I was a small town guy from Durham, NC, driving this great piece of Italian machinery. I figured that was as grown up, and at the same time, as kid-like as I was ever going to get. It's a wonderful thing to have and drive great cars. It doesn't make me the baddest mofo in the valley. It just means I've got a great piece of automotive art. And it's so much fun to drive!

Money can buy you moments of pleasure, decadence and bliss. But they are only moments in time. Money can't buy you love and it can't make you feel good about yourself, if you didn't feel good about yourself in the first place. It's nothing more than an empty seduction. The belief that "I'll be happy when I've got more money" is ludicrous.

Money is fun! But it's not the whole deal. It's what's inside of you that creates contentment or lack thereof. It's not the money. Money can add to the richness of your experiences. If you want to go meditate on a mountaintop in Tibet, having a lot of money does make it a lot easier to get there.

Just about everyone loves the idea of having a lot of money. Yet we've heard so many stories about people with money being miserable. Why are there so many miserable rich people? It's because they become the money. They let it take over their lives. They see it only as a vehicle to protect, not to enjoy; to acquire more, not to use what they have for good. The pursuit of money becomes an obsession and they lose all sense of balance and all too often they lose their sense of ethics and values as well. They don't see having money as an opportunity; they see it as a fortress against the world. It isolates them.

I know a lot of miserable rich people, but I also know a lot of happy rich people. Look at people like Bill Gates and his wife Melinda. Look at Oprah. These are really, really wealthy people who go out and do great things with their money. Those people and a lot of other people just like them do so much good in the world. One of the nicest things about having money is the ability to give some away. That is probably the most rewarding part about being rich. People who hoard their money really miss the boat. There is so much joy in sharing good fortune. It's hard to be miserable when you are making a difference in people's lives and having a positive impact in the world.

The happiest people I ever met in my life are in Bali—they don't have anything in a material sense, but they are happy because of deep spiritual beliefs. They surround themselves with art and music.

They're just blissfully happy. Most of them are the poorest people I've ever been around yet they live in a beautiful place. Being poor in Bali and being poor in Calcutta are real different. It's what you are surrounded by and how you view the world internally that makes the difference.

I have spent a lot of energy in my life trying not to be some rich jerk. It seems that people expect me to be one because I'm rich. Money doesn't make me or any other rich person better than anybody else. It just gives me more freedom and a broader range of choices.

A person's got to understand what money brings and what it doesn't bring. Money can be a nice addition to your life because it can buy you lots of fun things. What's important in life, to my way of thinking is the love and health of family and friends. These are constants. If I had to make a choice between having the love and good health of family or having a lot of money, I'd choose love, happiness and good health any day. You can have all the money in the world and still have the doctor tell you that you have cancer and you'll die in six months. The money doesn't mean a hell of a lot then.

Behind the Scenes with Barrie

Guess Who's Coming to Dinner
Dining at Michael Jackson's

Being somewhat of a mover and shaker in the music industry afforded me some extraordinary opportunities to rub shoulders with the rich and famous. I'm a consummate people watcher. I've been able to observe first hand the foibles and idiosyncrasies behind the celebrity screen. Celebrity does not make you superhuman. In fact celebrity often challenges you to stay in reality. Take Michael Jackson.

Back in his glittering King of Pop days, I was fortunate to be on the A-list of invitees to a dinner at Michael Jackson's Encino home near Los Angeles. No expense was spared to herald the arrival of his much-anticipated album, *Bad*. Epic Records flew in a few of the top retailers in the country to be among the first people to hear the album. My wife Arlene, and I, like just about everyone else, were starstruck over Michael Jackson. It was indeed one of the highlights of my career in the music business.

The event began at the very elegant and posh Beverly Hills Hotel. Walter Yetnikoff, the CEO of CBS Records at the time, unveiled the album for us at the hotel. With a pomp and circumstance befitting the King of Pop, we were indeed regaled by the music. I liked the album a lot, though I'm easily bribed by good food and wine, and this was major bribery. They poured Cristal Champagne all night, my first experience with what I now consider to be the greatest champagne in the world. As an aside, I got rip roaring drunk but I managed to retain a lot of the extraordinary memories from that evening. Following the recital, we were shuttled by limo out to Michael's house for dinner, where the celebrated chef Wolfgang Puck, of Spago fame, was preparing our meal.

As we approached the gate of the house, I was astounded by the sight of 20 or 30 kids camped out on the corner. Apparently they stayed there all the time just waiting for Michael to come and go.

I had seen hero worship before, but I'd never seen anything like that. Of the entire evening, that's my most vivid memory. I wondered why anybody would want to sit on a corner to wait to see somebody come out in a car. It revealed a mind-boggling obsession with the King of Pop.

The first thing I noticed when we got out of the limo were the two giraffes. I had never seen a giraffe at someone's house before. I'm talking real giraffes. I expected to meet Bubbles the monkey, but the giraffes were a surprise. The gardens carried out the zoo theme with a myriad of trees sculpted into exotic animal shapes. This wasn't even Neverland—just a home in a quiet upper class neighborhood in Encino. It was big, it was nice and it was tasteful.

Once inside, we found a curious mix of the ordinary and the extraordinary. We were not allowed in the living chambers upstairs so I can't confirm or deny all those rumors about Michael having an iron lung or many of the other bizarre things attributed to him at the time. I did get to meet the monkey. Remember when he used to carry Bubbles around with him everywhere he went? Then he stopped carrying the monkey around and replaced him with various children in tow. We were there before Webster replaced the monkey.

When we first entered the house, Michael wasn't around, but the monkey was. Michael came out and the monkey grabbed onto him. They let us wander around the entire bottom level of the house plus the guesthouse. The house itself was tastefully decorated with nice furniture. There were typical living areas, a nice kitchen—all the ordinary rooms you'd expect in a house.

But there was one huge room that was an entire arcade with every imaginable state-of-the-art video game and pinball machine. It was a step up from any commercial arcade that I had ever seen, and it was obviously set up for a whole bunch of people, except there was only one person living there. I assumed he entertained guests that included young people. It was a child's wonderland with all kinds of candy machines, win-a-toy machines—everything you would expect in an arcade, but quite unbelievable to find in someone's home. Arcades aren't the fad they used to be because kids have all the hand-held and home video game systems, but back then, this was a big deal.

The second most extraordinary thing about the house was in the guesthouse; there was a room with a couple of walls of decoupage featuring pictures with Michael Jackson and everybody in the world. I mean everybody. Presidents, Popes, diplomats, world leaders, movie stars, music people—you name it; they were up on that wall. I couldn't come up with a name of a famous person that wasn't there. Everybody wanted to have his or her picture taken with Michael Jackson.

I had seen some pretty impressive vanity walls before, but this one was the first one where it was sort of turned around, where everybody wanted to have their picture taken with the guy whose wall I was looking at. It was a real juxtaposition. I suppose the President of the United States could have a more impressive vanity wall, but there wouldn't be many people on Earth that could. By comparison, a president's term lasts only 4-8 years, whereas, Michael's mystique has lasted a lifetime.

The combination of seeing the kids camped out at the corner and viewing his photo gallery left me with an overwhelming appreciation for the magnitude of this guy's fame. It hit me that Michael was in a different league of celebrity. His popularity was immense—he had this Pied Piper thing going, where little kids, teenagers and maybe even adults wanted to follow him around. He may have been the most recognizable person in the world at the time. I don't care who you are, that kind of fame is going to change you. That kind of personal power and following, can, in the worst circumstance create someone who thinks they are omnipotent. I think that's what happened to Michael.

Michael Jackson was bigger than life. He was, after all, The King of Pop. People who worked for him were in awe of him. Anything Michael wanted, they would make happen. No one questioned Michael or second-guessed him. There was no one that said, "Michael, this might not be in your best interest." We all need a sounding board, a safe place to take ideas and an avenue that provides us with feed back. Without that we have the capacity to lose touch with reality.

Michael lives a fantasy life that is so far removed from what any of us can relate to. I'm not apologizing for him, but we can't relate to the reality of his existence. You take just a little bit of craziness, and fame is going to magnify it. You take a whole lot of craziness, and you've got somebody who's just off the charts in terms of living in reality.

This kind of fame, popularity, power and money is going to make anybody a little nutty. That's if somebody's fairly normal. You take a guy like Michael Jackson who was nuts to start with because of his family background, and you get a guy who has no connection to reality in the world.

I met his father at dinner that night—Joe Jackson's eyes were the scariest eyes of anybody I ever met. I've met two people in my life whose eyes just scared the living hell out of me—and the other was Jerry Lee Lewis, also known as "The Killer."

There are situations that happen to people that they cannot be prepared for. Without a lot of support and the occasional person to say "this is crazy" or "no, don't do this," it is very easy to spiral out of control. The people with decent family upbringing who have something normal to move back towards can usually pull it together, but God help you if you don't have a normal place to find sanity.

Given the famous people I've been around, I know for an absolute fact that I don't want to be famous. You give up way too much of yourself. I would prefer being able to go to dinner and know I can have a quiet evening with my wife or my friends without people coming up in the middle of a meal and asking me for an autograph or stopping me on the street. Being famous gets you a good table in a restaurant and good seats in a theater, but it's not worth it. I'd just rather be rich. I'd take rich any day over famous.

Part II:

No Donalds Allowed

Chapter 6

Don't Defecate Where You Live
Creating a fun place to work

When I first started managing a record store, I was 21 years old and just out of college. I developed a lot of theories fairly early on. The first thing I decided is that you do not crap where you live. Meaning, if I had to be there, why not create an environment that feels good and is fun? When work felt great, I was happy and much more productive. So it was easy to extrapolate that if my employees felt great and were having fun, we'd be a more productive team.

Anything you can do to encourage a fun atmosphere in a business is a good idea. The perfect example of this is Southwest Airlines. They are in a serious business. The serious thing about airplanes is that you need to keep them up in the air. I mean if they come down, that ruins everybody's day. They need to be flown by competent people; they need to be fixed by competent people; and they need to have competent people on the ground. But at the same time the guy at the top, Herb Kelleher, has created a fun work environment for the company. If you are on their airplanes or on the ground, people are always joking around. Everything's not so deadly serious. Even in the heightened security age we are living in, at Southwest Airlines it feels like people are having a good time. It translates to the customer, and it certainly translates to the bottom line. While all the other airlines were just absolutely going down the toilet, Southwest Airlines continued to thrive. I think it is a direct result of the atmosphere that has been created from the top down.

Now I think it's probably hard to build a fun atmosphere in a coal mine, so I will grant you that some situations might be pretty challenging. But even in a coal mine, management could make a point to take the men out for a beer after they resurface. There are ways that management can make a tough situation better while improving morale, even in the most God-awful circumstances.

At Record Bar we used to have an office wide mixer on Friday afternoons. We called it the Other Meeting. It was actually a cocktail party. Attendance was optional, but nearly everyone in the office came. It was an opportunity for people from all departments to meet and socialize. New employees were individually introduced at that time, and if someone was having a birthday, there'd be a birthday cake. If anybody called during that time, the switchboard would just say that person was at the Other Meeting. We encouraged people to talk to each other.

We hosted an annual company convention. It was held in great locations like Hilton Head, Nashville, and Los Angeles. All of our store managers and their spouses or significant others attended this four day party with great food and major entertainment –entertainment like Jimmy Buffett, Alabama, Joan Baez, Vince Gill, and Lionel Ritchie. Our suppliers, the record labels, participated by showcasing new products and helping to pay for these events.

Fun can be created in many ways. In our office, we kept the atmosphere light. Dress style and hair length in our warehouse and office were at the individual's discretion. We had to be somewhat careful in stores, so we didn't offend our customers. Music played everywhere in our office, and people could do whatever they wanted to their workspace. We had one guy who stuck hundreds of pencils in the ceiling. I still don't know why.

We also had no rules about social interaction. It was fine with management if people in the company dated each other. I think it's absolutely ridiculous for management to try to legislate relationships. You can't stop it anyway, and it's stupid to try. If you enjoy spending time with someone and you're comfortable with them, it's natural to develop a relationship. Work is a far better environment than a dark smoke-filled bar to meet someone.

My wife Arlene, our VP of Human Resources at Record Bar, had a big machine that dispensed M&Ms in her office. She would draw a steady stream of people into her office, and they would often sit down to talk. A lot of companies would see that as a total time waster, but it wasn't. That's how you get to know people. I think the VP of Human Resources needs to get to know people. That's a good thing. We used to call her the Head Human.

Arlene and I were in it for the fun. It never occurred to us that we were going to get rich. We were just trying to make a living and have fun in the process.

My parents worked together, and Arlene's did also. They became role models for us. As we observed their interactions, we learned what to do and what not to do in making a business relationship work. I don't think they ever enjoyed their work as much as we did.

When we were just starting out, we thought that having 5 stores would be the most wonderful thing in the world, but probably unattainable. Then 10 stores happened. We continued to set new goals, and our company continued to grow. Our attitude was always positive. We knew that however successful or unsuccessful our business decisions were, we'd be okay because we had each other.

The key to our success in working together was the set of agreements we had with each other:

• *The buck stopped with me*. It's important in any business to come to an understanding on how decisions will be made. Otherwise, you can have a company with unlimited potential that goes nowhere very fast. Making no decision is a decision, often a bad decision. Being the President of the company, I took the responsibility for having the final say.

• *Business discussions stayed in the office*. We traveled for business extensively as the company grew. Also, most of our closest friends worked for Record Bar. Our time at home with our family and friends was special. There was no rehashing of what went wrong during the day.

• *I didn't have the stomach for insurance settlements*. It used to make me sick when we'd catch a shoplifter, and the customer would turn around and sue us for false arrest or whatever ridiculous charge they could make against us. Even though they were caught red-handed, our insurance company would end up paying them off, just to avoid going to court. I asked Arlene not to tell me about those situations. One claim against us was rather amusing to me . . . a warehouse employee was fired due to poor performance. She sued the company stating that she was fired because she was fat and Jewish. Apparently she had never met *me*.

• *We operated on a need to know basis*. There were numerous times when I had information that did not impact Arlene or her department directly. So, I didn't tell her. As VP of Human Resources, Arlene knew who had AIDS, who was getting a divorce, and who was delinquent with child support. I never knew any of this information. We both respected confidentiality.

Working together was full of challenges. We didn't always agree, but we always respected and loved each other. We stayed married because we worked on our relationship.

In the entertainment business that saw relationships as a throw-away, we stayed together, and we were both rewarded for our efforts. Now after 45 years of marriage the work of the early years is replaced by an effortless lightness in our relationship. However, if Charlize Theron calls . . .

I believe that having fun in any business is essential. It cannot be cultivated in a negative environment. The environment has to change first. A strong organizational ethical base must be in place, and people have to treat each other with respect. Only then can it be experienced. Fun works for me on several levels, but from a hard-core business perspective, having fun contributes to the bottom line. Not only can you have fun while making a profit, your profits will be more abundant if you are having fun along the way.

Chapter 7

He Said She Said
Squelching the gossip mill

I've seen just about all the corporate games people play. In my experience, "He Said She Said" was the one most played and the one most deadly to the individual and to the organization. The game goes like this. John says to Mary that Jane is screwing up. Then Mary immediately goes to Bob and says that she heard that Jane is screwing up. Pretty soon, you've got a widely held perception that Jane is a screw up. It happens all the time. The gossip mill shreds a person's reputation. Often there's no merit to the accusation. It is the worst kind of organizational politics. It's divisive communication, and it's amazing how many organizations accept it. If nothing is done, this kind of communication can create an organizational nightmare with no relation to any truth.

The only way to stop the game is on a person-to-person level. People have to understand that it's a terrible way to communicate and that it's unacceptable in the organization. When there's an issue between two or more people, the most effective way to resolve it is for those involved to discuss it among themselves and come up with a resolution. The way I chose to stop it in our organization was to start with what I could affect personally. The people who worked for me knew that if they came into my office to criticize somebody's behavior or decision, they would have to face that person with me in my office. They'd have to say it to their face, not behind their back. If necessary, I'd facilitate, but we would talk it out, all three of us, and the issue would get resolved.

Most people didn't like that. Generally, people will go to great lengths to avoid confrontation. Not surprisingly, once the person who was the subject of the gripe joined us in the office, the one with the issue would clam up. It would take some coaxing on my part, but once the dialogue started, what appeared a huge issue at the outset became an opportunity for deeper understanding. These were reasonable, competent, hardworking people. We found you could always talk it out and reach a resolution, if the issue was out in the open. It's when "He Said She Said" is left unaddressed that great damage is done.

If you want your people to adopt a certain behavior, you've got to model it at the top. In my executive management group we made an agreement—if you say something to anybody in the group, you're saying it to everybody. I don't believe in secrets anyway, because my experience is people don't keep secrets. So there's no point in having them. Immediately the alarm goes off when somebody says "I'm going to tell you, but don't tell anyone else." My philosophy has always been, "Say it to me, you've said it to everybody. Don't say it to me if you don't want everybody to know!" It cut out a lot of the crap!

Everyone understood that I expected our organization to have an open and honest, way of communicating with each other. If you are going to be open and honest you also have to be careful about the way you say things. People seem to have difficulty separating the person from the offending opinion or point of view. There is a big difference between, "I disagree with you because you are a scumbag" and "I disagree with your concept." There are ways to disagree and get the point across, without it being a personal attack.

People should tell each other what they think. Usually in organizations that's not what they do. As a manager, if I don't agree with what you are saying or like what you are doing or disapprove of the way you are doing it, I believe I have an ethical obligation to bring it to your attention. But I don't have to start calling you names—to your face or especially behind your back. I believe it is always best to say what you have to say directly to the person involved. Just be careful and tactful about how you say it.

Let's talk about how it works on a peer level. If we disagree, there have to be ground rules. First of all, if we disagree, you don't run off and do character assassination on me to somebody else. Secondly, if we disagree and the organization makes the decision that your viewpoint is the one we are going to adopt, it's important that I get on board and not just continue to beat that dead horse.

There are times that you may disagree with a decision that is made, but ranting and raving about it is never appropriate in the workplace. It is disruptive and obnoxious. A discussion with your immediate supervisor may provide a better understanding of why or how the decision was made. But keep in mind, the workplace is not a democracy. The guy at the top gets to make the final call. If he or she is a good leader, he gets input from employees. He gathers all of the information and hopefully makes the correct decision.

Once people understood what I was advocating, they really liked it. They understood that "He Said She Said" was a divisive and destructive game and it wasted a lot of time and energy that could be put to better use. Over time, the behavior stopped.

Chapter 8

357 Magnum Style Management
Managing by intimidation

In a company or in an organization, a manager's job is to get people to do things that are good for the organization and also good for the individual. As a manager I have a lot of latitude in how I choose to treat my subordinate.

A really good manager will figure out the specific style that is most effective in motivating an employee to do what needs to be done. Unfortunately, too many managers think the style that works best is what I call the "357 Magnum Style of Management."

The way this style works is, I point a 357 Magnum at my subordinate and say, "Dance." A huge majority of people faced with this directive will immediately join the American Ballet Theater. They make their best efforts to dance with grace, aesthetics and technical acumen. As long as I continue to point that Magnum at them, they will continue to dance.

Unfortunately, this style only works as long as I am standing over them. Guess what happens when I've got to go to the bathroom? They stop dancing. And when they stop dancing, and I'm not there to observe, they are usually pretty pissed off.

I see a lot of managers who adopt the 357 Magnum style. They are some mean hombres. They are tough on their folks. They are disciplinarians, martinets. Their style works extremely well in the short term. But the problem is they are creating a dangerous undercurrent of discontent. Just like evil kings throughout history have created rebellion in their kingdoms, someone mean enough in a corporate structure will create a rebellion among the personnel. Eventually people figure out how to bring down the manager and, ultimately, the organization that is creating their misery.

Fear and intimidation is an oppressive management style that encourages bad behavior and poor performance. It creates passive-aggressive employees. Some people go as far as sabotage; others seek employment opportunities elsewhere, neither of which is in the best interests of the company.

Other styles are more effective in the long term. There are ways to get people to do their jobs that don't involve fear and threats. My experience is that positive reinforcement in word and deed works best.

The style of management that I endorse is what I call Management by Inclusion. I want people to feel like they have input, that they are heard, that their ideas are valued, and that somebody cares enough about what they are saying to really listen. Allow them a say in how they do their job. People are most effective in their work when they feel valued as an individual and when they believe that the organization cares about them.

If you are micromanaging and holding a gun, your subordinates are never going to offer their ideas. They will just lay low and watch the clock. People don't work very well in an atmosphere of fear.

Most people want to do a good job. They want to succeed. They want to do what will further their careers. But, if you discover that there are too many people who don't succeed, it's probably an indication that you should take a closer look at the effectiveness of your management style.

Chapter 9

Who Gets The Credit?
Leave your ego at the door

If I had to pick one area where I feel American business has lost its way, it would be in the sanctioning of political in-fighting and cutthroat tactics among co-workers. It has become all about who gets the credit. The idea that it's a good thing to claw your way to the top, leaving bodies strewn in your path, just astounds me. What a miserable way to do business, and what a losing strategy.

Look at the Donald Trump television show: "The Apprentice". That's not the way I want my people to compete—by trying to hurt each other. That's exactly the opposite of how I want a company to run. If there were a primer on what not to do, "The Apprentice" would be it. I could enjoy watching "The Apprentice", if it was just a TV program, but it reflects an unfortunate reality in much of the business world where managers pit people against each other. It's not an effective or pleasant style. It certainly doesn't work as effectively as having everyone pulling together as a team.

An inordinate amount of time and energy in organizations is taken up by people jockeying for credit. When people feel the only way to further their career is at the expense of fellow employees, the environment becomes toxic. The rush to take credit creates resentment, anger and dysfunction, completely stripping away the possibility of effective teamwork. If an organization is going to function properly, you can't condone people taking credit at someone else's expense.

My view is that if the organization wins, the individual wins. Therefore, it is not all that important who gets credit for what. In order to work for the good of the group, an employee has got to believe he or she will be rewarded for their contribution. Using reverse logic, if people in a corporate structure feel they have to be concerned whether they are going to get credit all the time, it says they believe they won't get rewarded for their contribution.

Recognition of the contribution of an individual or a team is a strong motivator. To create an organization that rewards the individual, you have to incentivize people for teamwork, and pay them well for their contribution. But it can't just be about the money. Recognition by the company and/or their peer group is also vitally important. It is paramount that they get enough ego strokes to feel good about what they are doing. Corporate pats on the back go a long way with people.

Individual contributions are what make a team successful. Being a team player means working really hard toward the goal that helps the organization succeed. Sometimes this means an individual gives up some personal recognition for the sake of the team. But that doesn't mean you can never be a star. There are star performers within a team too. But they are stars in different ways. They are stars because they really want to see the company succeed, and they are confident that if the company succeeds, they will be taken care of.

A great analogy for corporate teamwork is to look at the dynamics of a basketball team. A guy on a fast break down the court passes the ball to a guy who scores. The chances of the guy scoring off the pass are 60%. The chances of the first guy scoring if he didn't pass are 40%. So the team is better off because he gave up possible personal glory for good of the team. He didn't get the stat in his column, but the team gained 2 points. Would you rather average 20 points a game with a team that wins half its games, or 10 points a game in a team that wins all its games?

You see teamwork in sports and you see it in the movie business. Look at the Academy Awards ceremony. You hear it over and over, "I want to thank my producer, my director, my mother, my hairdresser..." It's about acknowledging that other people are a part of a successful venture.

There is never a star without a supporting cast. Organizations don't score big wins without a lot of people pulling together. Any time you get a corporate star, it's best to remember that a lot of people are making contributions behind the scenes. Ideas rarely come from just one person; they tend to germinate among a bunch of people. Inevitably if one person gets credit, one person is happy and three are pissed. I'd rather have four people happy. It's the team as a whole and each contributor within that deserves to get credit.

One of the most impressive demonstrations of teamwork I've ever witnessed was during the production of the song, "We Are The World." Harry Chapin, who was a good friend of mine, came up with the idea of a star-studded extravaganza to raise money for world hunger. After he died, a bunch of us came together to carry out the concept. The recording session was a gathering of more than 25 of the biggest names in entertainment at the time: Stevie Wonder, Bruce Springsteen, Michael Jackson, Diana Ross, Billy Joel, Lionel Ritchie, Cindi Lauper, The Pointer Sisters — and the list went on and on. Quincy Jones was producing it. He put a sign up on the recording studio door that said, "Leave Your Egos at the Door." Everybody shut up and listened to him. They started at 9 p.m. and didn't finish until dawn. As a united team, passionate about their cause, they melded into one harmonious voice, and produced an incredible song in a single night.

If you can do that in a corporate environment, or any other environment, everyone's a star, everybody wins and we all get the credit.

Chapter 10

Firing Someone Is Never Easy
Procrastinating only makes it harder

As a corporate executive, the hardest thing I ever had to do was to fire an employee. The words, "You're fired" have become a catch phrase in TV entertainment. This incenses me. Firing someone is not fun. If firing someone gets easy, I believe there is something wrong with you. It may be the right thing to do, but it really sucks to have to do it.

I would get a feeling in the pit of my stomach when I knew somebody had to go. I would try to ignore it or prove it wrong, but the feeling never changed. And whether I fired them the next day, the next week or the next year, it always came to pass. So eventually I realized that once I got that feeling, the best way to proceed was to let the person go and to do it as quickly as possible.

I'm not some heartless bastard, who enjoys cutting off people's heads. But there are times when people just can't make the grade. If someone is not right for the organization, inevitably, the organization is not right for him or her either. It's better for the individual to move on and to have a chance to find a better fit where they can feel happy and appreciated for their contribution.

Of course nobody ever wants to get fired. In the moment, you are never going to hear anyone say, "Oh thank you so much! I know this is best for me!" Getting fired is an emotionally painful experience. That's why I developed strategies to make the experience as quick and succinct as possible. Firing someone is not a time for a lengthy discussion or rehashing what went wrong. It's a time to deliver your decision as a fait accompli.

Over time, I realized that in the process of firing someone, I couldn't teach them anything. There is no point in offering any parting words of wisdom. Nobody's going to hear them anyway. The only thing that will register is the fact they have just lost their job. So I decided when I had to fire someone, I wouldn't get into any detailed explanations, discussions or arguments.

I think exit interviews can be effective as a feedback mechanism, but only when someone is leaving on their own accord. An exit interview with somebody who is getting fired will be distorted and rarely useful because it will be colored with anger, hurt, and sour grapes. So if you have to fire someone, just do it and get it over with.

The worst moments of my entire managerial career were in situations where I was firing someone and they cried. That happened a few times. If I could have, I would have dug a hole in the floor and crawled in. I empathized with their feelings more than any of these people could have imagined. Sometimes I even cried too. I tried not to. I never, ever found it easy to tell someone they had to go.

I developed a set of informal rules for firing someone. They may not be for everyone but it certainly helped me in a very difficult situation. First, I always fired somebody in their office, never in mine — so I could do it and get the hell out of there. That probably sounds cowardly and maybe it is, but the truth is, it does no one any good to prolong the agony. There was nothing else to be accomplished.

I could try to assuage hurt feelings, but experience taught me that I couldn't even do that.

Second, I would wait until late in the day, even after hours if I thought I could manage it. As much as possible, I wanted to avoid the humiliation of having their co-workers witness the event. Third, I would never arrange a meeting ahead of time because I didn't want them to have to think about it all day. I did it when I could find somebody in his or her office. Unfortunately this brought on a sort of cat and mouse game a few times when I went to fire somebody and they weren't there. Once I couldn't find a guy for three days!

My experience was that firings never came as a surprise to anybody. When somebody was screwing up, everybody knew it including the person being fired. If you are doing your job properly as a manager, you are providing regular feedback, so a person should never be truly surprised when they are fired for poor performance.

I don't believe in lame ducks. When people are fired, they should go immediately. I'd pay them severance and try to be fair, but I would ask them to leave. It was better for the morale of the organization to move on quickly. I always had somebody ready to step in to make the transition as smooth as possible.

After firing someone, I would always meet with the people in the affected department as quickly as I could get them together, so I could manage the information flow. This made it easier to settle down any organizational turmoil after the word got out. In a void, all kinds of rumors will develop as to why somebody had to go. It's best to allow people a chance to ask questions and to vent their feelings.

Without a doubt, firing someone was the toughest single thing that I ever had to do in business. And I hope to God I never have to do it again. There were a few times I should have fired myself. I thought about it. But I was usually able to right my ship by having a stern talk with myself. That's the nice thing about being a CEO. You don't usually fire yourself.

Behind the Scenes with Barrie

Moments to Remember
Meeting extraordinary people

I've spent many years in the entertainment business, so I've had a lot of opportunities to come in contact with celebrities. I'm an observer at heart and I'm a student of human behavior, so observing celebrity behavior is particularly fun for me.

The most extraordinary celebrity I ever met was Harry Chapin. He was a very talented singer, songwriter, poet, and playwright. But what impressed me the most was that Harry was totally dedicated to trying to save the world. Today we have many stars helping to raise money for cause after cause, so perhaps it sounds like it's no big deal. But when Harry was doing it, back in the 70's, it was a big deal.

Harry played more unpaid concerts than paid ones by a ratio of 2:1. If you could come up with an idea about damn near anything that was a good cause, he'd play your concert. He would fly all over the place on his dime to help raise money. He helped create the World Hunger Organization. He and Bob Geldof put together *We Are The World*, and organized huge concerts all over the world to raise money for world hunger.

Inexplicably, Harry died very young and I still miss the hell out of him. He left behind his wife and six kids. He had a huge heart. I often think of him when I try to do something good for somebody. But it would take a whole lot of me, and a lot of many other people, to replace Harry Chapin. He set the bar for using celebrity to make a difference in the world.

* * *

More often than not, celebrities have a reputation for being egomaniacs. I was pleased to make the acquaintance of a number of wonderful exceptions. Years ago at Record Bar we had a room set up for employees to do martial arts or whatever physical activities they wanted to do. The room was big enough to use for informal concerts. The room was essentially a corner in our warehouse. It wasn't Carnegie Hall, but it was an adequate space for musicians to play.

We asked this new artist who was just starting out in his career to come to our warehouse and play for us. Even though nobody had ever heard of him, our entire company fell in love with him and his music that day. It was Lyle Lovett. He's one of the all-time nicest guys—smart and funny with a warm personality. Lyle sang most of his first album, including the song "Closing Time" and "Pony on My Boat," which was on a later record. Lyle was by himself with a guitar, and he was absolutely mesmerizing.

Later, when I taught at the University of North Carolina, Lyle came and spoke to my class. I found out he was getting a PHD at Texas A & M, when he decided to become a musician, so he was totally comfortable in a classroom setting.

We watched his career skyrocket; he became a huge star. Lyle's a perfect example that nice guys do indeed finish first!

* * *

Female music artists especially tend to get saddled with a reputation for being difficult divas. Once again I found a delightful exception. When I was the President of the National Association of Recording Merchandisers, we attended a celebrity-packed party as part of our annual convention. The party was held in two adjacent rooms. When we arrived, we were introduced to Loretta Lynn. She was sensational—down-home, country and very nice—just Loretta. She was wearing this knockout red dress. It was stunning and elegant and you couldn't miss noticing it.

We talked to her awhile and thoroughly enjoyed her company. Later, Arlene and I wandered off into the other room to mingle with the other guests. We weren't there long when we saw another woman wearing the same gorgeous red dress that Loretta was wearing. Arlene and I looked at each other and said, "Uh oh, maybe we ought to go tell Loretta." We found Loretta and told her, expecting that she'd be upset to hear the news. To our utter surprise, Loretta said, "Well isn't that nice! Come on, let's go talk to her!" And she went in and introduced herself to this woman. When we left they were having an animated conversation. It was just a wonderful moment.

Truly powerful people are not intimidated by imitation. Her ego could handle it. She was comfortable in her own skin being Loretta Lynn. The accoutrement of a dress didn't define her as a person.

* * *

Sam Kinison was one of the wildest comedians around, which is extraordinary because he was trained as a preacher. My daughter Janis was backstage after one of his shows and was introduced to him. When Sam heard who Janis' father was, he was very excited. He got down on his knees and kissed her feet. Ain't Rock n' Roll wonderful?

* * *

I was at a music business picnic in Macon, GA. I was being introduced to a group of people, when I suddenly realized that I had just been introduced to Bette Midler. She was dressed in a sweatshirt and jeans and was very quiet. She was a long way from the persona she created for herself. I spent the next hour or so playing pool with her and Martin Mull. She made an impression on me because there was not much star there – just a regular person.

* * *

My experience of meeting a lot of celebrities is that most of them are nice folks and they are reasonably comfortable in their skin. Some of the biggest stars I've ever met are some of the nicest people—like George Harrison and Willie Nelson—just wonderful people.

Of course, I have run across a number of not so nice celebrities. It has been my experience that just because you are a successful musician, it doesn't exempt you from the truth that "what goes around comes around." The stars I met who were jerks eventually faded from view. It hurt their careers. Fortunately, I haven't had that many unpleasant experiences with recording artists, but the bad encounters I have had were memorable.

* * *

A lot of celebrities struggle with substance abuse. Some manage to kick it and others don't. In 1964 Johnny Cash played the Jubilee concert series at the University of North Carolina. He was emerging from being a country music star to a much bigger pop star, but he wasn't there yet. He had just started performing with June Carter, who later became his wife. After the concert, Arlene and I went backstage and met Johnny. I was enthralled with him, a truly larger than life figure. At the time, he was struggling with major drug problems. I had heard he was doing a hundred hits of speed a day. That's hard to imagine.

Arlene and I had our picture taken with him. We stood on either side of him with Johnny in the middle. After we took the picture, Arlene and I both looked at each other and asked, "Did you feel that?" His hands were shaking as though he was making snow angels on our backs. Thank God he was able to kick the habit. It's amazing he was able to live as long and as healthy a life as he did. Not many people make it through that kind of addiction.

* * *

Phil Walden grew up very poor in Macon, Georgia and became a major player in the music industry. He was a musical genius, building Capricorn Records into a huge entertainment conglomerate, discovering Otis Redding, The Allman Brothers, Marshall Tucker, The Elvin Bishop Band, Widespread Panic, Cake, and many other great musicians.

Since we both grew up in the South in families of modest means, and ended up in the same business, naturally we gravitated toward each other and became good friends. He and his wife Peggy let us use their house in Hilton Head, South Carolina. Arlene and I later bought a home there because we fell in love with the island. We spent many great nights with the Waldens in semi-altered states.

When Jimmy Carter ran for president, Phil's bands raised money for his campaign. Carter was a Georgia peanut farmer with few resources, and Phil was instrumental in financing Carter's campaign. The President never forgot Phil's work, and he and Phil maintained a close friendship.

We made mutual friends in the White House through Phil and were invited there many times. Phil introduced us to top White House staffers as well as many celebrities who performed at various functions there. These events were some of the most exciting experiences of my life.

Years later Phil's drinking and drugging got the best of him. He lost his company, all of his money, and most of his friends. Near the bottom of his downward spiral he called me one day and said he had a chance to make a major deal that could put him back in the big time. He needed $75,000.

I had misgivings, but I couldn't turn my back on my friend. Arlene and I signed a note for Phil because we certainly didn't have $75,000 to loan him. Unfortunately, the deal didn't work and we had to pay the note off. It was hard; we didn't have that much money then.

Phil went bankrupt and the IRS sold all of his assets for back taxes. It was awful. A proud man and a great businessman was humiliated. I didn't hear much from him, but I did know that he went through rehab and joined AA.

Arlene and I were in Hilton Head a few years later. We were taking a walk on the beach, when I saw a flash of Phil Walden running off the beach. It was obvious that he was embarrassed about seeing us. I was so upset that not only had I lost my money, but I also lost my friend. I wrote Phil a letter telling him of my dismay and charged the experience off to one of life's lessons.

One day a year later my assistant called me in my office and asked me if I would take a phone call from Phil Walden. I said, "Sure." When I got on the phone, Phil apologized to me and said it was one of the worst things he had ever done in his life, and asked if he could make amends.

Phil was a good person, but even good people screw up. Phil screwed up big time. Turns out Phil had a conscience. He cared about others, and he knew that he had hurt many friends in his quest for success. When good people make mistakes, it bothers them. It bothered Phil. His real success came as he made amends and turned his life around. His actions restored my faith in mankind.

* * *

I was at an LA Lakers game, and I sat with a friend, who had the same front row seats under the basket that Jack Nicholson has on the sideline. At halftime everyone in these seats walks onto the court and stands around like at a cocktail party. It's definitely *see and be seen* time.

I was in a group of people and was introduced to Don Rickles. People started drifting off, and suddenly it was just Rickles and me. I realized he was insulting me. It was the same machine gun delivery he used in his act. I guess he has become that person. I was honored to be his target. He also mentioned Frank a couple of times. This was the only conversation I ever had with anyone, who dropped Sinatra's name.

* * *

As CEO at Record Bar, one of the jobs I liked least was attending mall openings. They were long-winded affairs, full of speeches by politicians and developers patting themselves on the back. Once, however, I was at one in South Carolina where Gene Kelly was the featured speaker. He was a friend of the developer, and I guess he was picking up a few extra bucks.

When the ceremonies were over, I wandered around trying to find free food and drink, and I literally bumped into Mr. Kelly. He was by himself. And he looked as lost as I was. We chatted for a while, talked about movies and dancing. I was in heaven. He also told me that "Xanadu", the musical, was a terrible movie. He could not have been nicer.

* * *

Sex, drugs and rock 'n' roll. What they say is true. There are those celebrities who use sex to get where they want to go and it's so much a part of their M.O. that they keep on doing it after they are already famous.

I once got a call from a major female rock 'n' roll artist, a big star, who was promoting a new album. The interaction we had didn't have a hell of a lot to do with who I was, considering we had never met. She came on to me so strong over the telephone, I thought we were going to have phone sex! She later sent me a picture of her with a very suggestive inscription. She had a reputation for being out there and her album covers were always incredibly sexy. I've still never met her, but I sure would like to.

I once got a phone call from George Burns, but he didn't seem interested in having sex with me. He was just promoting a new record.

Celebrities are like everybody else, they just make more money and get more attention. Some are wonderful and some are awful, but most fall somewhere in the middle. It's sad that our society values singing, acting, and playing sports more than teaching and policing, but the marketplace is dynamic and maybe in a few years garbage collection will take its rightful place in People magazine's most beautiful professions.

Part III:

The Pyramid Starts at the Top

Chapter 11

Follow the Leader
Glance over your shoulder, is anyone
following?

I think leadership is the single most neglected concept in American business today. We spend a lot of time talking about management but we don't spend enough time talking about leadership. What's the difference you might ask? Management follows a direction set by someone else. Leadership sets that direction.

The leadership styles we normally think about are the larger than life military figures like Patton and Napoleon—tough guys with large egos and very dictatorial. In a military situation, that's a style that works pretty well. I don't have any problem with a leadership style that's dogmatic if it's effective. In fact, I don't have a problem with any leadership style that is ethical, honest and takes the followers to a place that's good for them and the organization. The reality is that different situations require different kinds of leadership.

It's easy to determine if you are a leader. Just glance over your shoulder. If there is anybody back there, you're a leader. Leaders develop followers. The way that leaders create themselves is by being charismatic and definitive, and by earning respect. A good leader figures out what style is going to work and develops that persona. People do not follow leaders unless they perceive them as strong.

Leadership and charisma-you can almost use them interchangeably—because leaders always have charisma. No matter what you think of Bill Clinton, that guy profiles totally as a leader. He's got charisma coming out of his pores. How do you define charisma? Hell, I don't know. You know people who've got it and people who don't.

Leadership can be a tremendous amount of fun. It's a nice stroke for your ego when people are following you. The problem is that not all leaders are good leaders. I have seen natural leaders with all the charisma in the world who would lead people into a wall. It does not help to get up to the top of the hill only to find out it's a sheer drop-off into the ravine.

Richard Nixon was a leader who found people to follow him. But look at who they were. They were scarier than hell and they cut him off from the entire country. Leaders need honest feedback from their followers. All Nixon heard is what his people chose to tell him, an effective leader doesn't want that.

A leader is out there in front. I don't believe in being a general who sits back on the hill and looks over the battle. I believe in leaders being out in front. In companies they're visible, they're aware of what's going on, and they're directing traffic.

Companies with great leaders have tremendous vision. Jack Welch is a perfect example. Look what he did with GE. Look at what Sam Walton did with Walmart. These people had tremendous vision and knew exactly where they were going. It was easy for them to rally the troops to implement their vision. Their followers would have gone through fire for them. That's what good leadership is about.

Sam Walton, by the force of his personality took a little tiny company and said, "We are going to give customers better service than anybody else." Better customer service meant cleaner stores and better prices. It meant hiring retired people to stand in front of the store to say hello, to be friendly and greet people. It meant a lot of different things. He set out to treat his customers better than anybody else. It was a rallying cry and a clear vision that inspired his people to follow.

Great leaders don't come along that often. You tend to get the management skill set over here, the charismatic lunatic over there, or you get someone who's got a clear idea where they are going, but just doesn't know how to get the troops there. You don't normally get the person with true vision who also has the charisma to lead. At least I haven't seen it much.

Leadership can be taught to people who have good personalities, but they must want to lead. The average Joe off the street is not interested in being followed. There's just too much responsibility involved. Both ethics and leadership principles should be taught in schools, but this is rarely done effectively.

Chapter 12

The Pyramid Theory
Good people beget good people

I believe organizations by their nature are pyramidal in form. The pyramid starts at the top and cascades down. The way the theory goes is that good people hire good people and the pyramid expands outward and downward. If done properly, a large organization can be built from top to bottom with people who share the values and ethics of the person at the very top of the pyramid.

I came to adopt this theory after years of observing how things worked at Record Bar. At our peak, we had over 200 stores located in 30 states. I could go into any of our stores and feel that the people working there were similar to me. They were younger of course, but their ideas, attitudes, and energy were similar to mine. I could go into the stores and feel comfortable they were carrying out my vision and representing our company in a way that made me proud.

My experience is that people tend to hire people who are like them. This creates a very homogeneous organization in terms of values, attitudes and beliefs. Taken to an extreme, the organization can lose the balance and perspective to be gained by embracing diversity. All people have their strengths and weaknesses. Managers tend to look for people who mirror their strengths and wind up with a lopsided crew. It is important to hire individuals who can fill in the gaps.

The challenge is different for different managers. Personally, I am a creative visionary, always looking into the future, but not into the details. I don't like dealing with day-to-day operational headaches. I tended to hire creative, outgoing, friendly people who weren't very good with details either. I realized after awhile, I couldn't keep hiring people who were just like me. Somebody somewhere has got to fill in the details!

It was a hard lesson for me to learn. It just wasn't intuitive to me. I was in a business that was based on art and creativity, so it just seemed natural to hire artsy creative types. Very quickly, I learned that I needed people who liked doing the routine kinds of things and could do them well. Somebody had to put cash in the register and somebody had to take it to the bank. We couldn't just have a bunch of music junkies sitting around listening to music all day.

I learned to value and seek diversity and not just diversity of skills. I wanted people to have different backgrounds representing a wide array of racial makeups, religious beliefs, and politics. I wanted both genders represented and some people who didn't fall neatly into either. It wasn't because I was trying to be politically correct. I believe diversity spawns innovation. Varying beliefs create more dialogue, which stimulates new thinking. If organizations get stuck in a rut thinking the same things over and over, and continue to operate the way they've always done, pretty soon they go the way of the buggy whip manufacturers. You become obsolete.

Diversity is good, with one exception. You want everyone on the same page in terms of values, ethics and goals. I believe the only way this can happen in an organization is when it is led by example from the very top of the pyramid. It can't work any other way. If you want an organization of hard workers who are competent and ethical, this had better be what is reflected in your management team.

Good people beget good people. Unfortunately, the converse is also true. If you hire one incompetent, then everybody below them in their section of the pyramid is incompetent as well. This underscores my belief that the most important decision that any organization ever makes is the hire. That's why it's so critical to get it right starting at the very top of the organization. If you are careful about the hire and you keep being careful all the way down the pyramid, you can create a fine organization. So it follows that if the CEO of an organization is a bad person, the organization isn't going to work. It may take a while for it to rear its ugly head, but it's coming. The pyramid starts at the top and cascades down. If you've got sludge at the top, you'll get sludge at the bottom.

Chapter 13

The Hiring Decision
Listening to Your Gut

The longer I was in business and the longer I ran a company, the more I realized the importance of hiring the right people. It's easy to talk about, and everybody gives lip service to hiring the right people, but it's a lot harder to do in practice.

Most managers are taught to hire from resumes. They look at qualifications on paper and decide whether the resume fits the job. Then they interview the person and make the hire—without regard for what makes the person tick. Personality dynamics are rarely considered. A person's got to have the qualifications, but the interaction between the manager and the potential hire is just as important. I also believe it is a mistake to delegate the hiring decision to the Human Resources department. HR doesn't have to live with this person every day. The hiring manager does. It's HR's responsibility to provide managers with qualified candidates. The manager's responsibility is to choose the candidate whose personality and energy best fits with the rest of the team.

In my early days as a manager, I hired a number of people who I really didn't like. They had excellent resumes with all the right experience, but I didn't have a good feeling about them. Without exception, down the road, these people turned out to be bad hires. I discovered it is vitally important to also take into account an individual's character and temperament before making a hiring decision.

After hiring enough of the wrong people, my first criteria became, "Do I like this person?" Perhaps that should be obvious, but how often do we ignore the red flags because a person looks good on paper? As I got better at hiring, I realized I could trust my intuitive sense about a person.

I think we have the world's greatest computer in our brains and the brain can process huge amounts of data very quickly. The intuitive hit we get, or gut reaction, is just the brain spitting out an answer after it's massaged a lot of data very quickly. I don't think any of us make enough use of that intuitive sense that we have. We are taught from childhood to think things through with reason and to ignore our first reaction. Learning to trust our intuition, with regard to people and decisions, creates better outcomes.

In time, I gave myself permission to listen to my gut instinct when hiring. I got better at picking people immediately. I made a rule that I was never going to hire anybody I didn't like. I didn't care how badly I needed to fill the spot. I would hold out for somebody I felt good about, and somebody always showed up that I liked and who was qualified.

A lot of managers will tell you they hire people they don't like because they've got the credentials. I think that's a mistake, you've got to have a certain kind of chemistry with your team if you want to create synergy. Unless I really liked them and got along with them, I couldn't manage them successfully. The person didn't have to be a stand-up comedian or a great personality to pass through my filter, just somebody I wanted to be around. Hiring someone you don't like is a disaster waiting to happen.

It's also important to assess whether the person you want to hire will enjoy working with you. There are two sides to the equation. I came within an inch of hiring a woman who had worked for Billy Graham to be my assistant. She was wonderful and would have been great for me. My concern was for her, and whether she could handle being around me. After all, I'm not as saintly as Billy. A good hiring fit works well for both parties.

I'm not suggesting you should hire somebody just because you enjoy his or her company. That's another lesson learned. I once hired a guy because he'd run a beauty pageant and had some great stories, really funny stories. I enjoyed the funny stories, but his job performance was lousy. Bad hire.

If you are going to rely on instincts, you'd better be sure your senses are neither compromised nor your judgment clouded by friendship. One time I hired someone I'd known for a long time. We had trouble setting up a formal interview because he couldn't get away from his job during the day, so I interviewed him one evening at my house. We sat around having cocktails. God that was stupid. Never make a hiring decision under the influence. Bad technique. Bad hire.

The way I got better at hiring the right people was by hiring an awful lot of wrong people. It was definitely an experiential game. There was a distinct learning curve. What I found was that when I hired the right people, I became a great manager.

Hiring decisions have long-term ramifications. Learning to trust my instincts about people has served me well in business. The right decisions always make your job easier, more fun and a whole lot less stressful. My advice is to always listen to your gut because the first answer is always the best answer.

Chapter 14

Organizations Owe Loyalty to People
Layoffs are a serious breach of trust

Of all the things I ever did as a manager, the one I regret most was laying off 18 employees during an economic downturn. I hated doing it and I believed it was wrong, but I let myself get talked into it. We built our company on a clearly understood set of values. The layoff was a mistake and a serious breach of trust. To this day, it hurts my conscience.

During this difficult time at Record Bar, we gave our department heads the choice of cutting salary by 20% or cutting out 20% of the employees. Several departments chose to cut salary. All of our top executives took a 20% decrease, including yours truly.

Given the chance, people will behave in heroic ways. The people who stayed worked their butts off to bring the company back to financial strength. As soon as we got back on our feet, we reinstated their salaries. Unfortunately, the people who were cut were not as easy to reinstate. More importantly, we lost the trust that loyalty would be repaid with loyalty.

I believe strongly that organizations owe loyalty to their employees as well as vice versa. There are better ways of cutting costs than just lopping off employees. This requires responsibility in organizations. You can't just cavalierly add massive amounts of people when times are good with the idea that you can get rid of them when times get tough.

My experience of watching how large companies operate is that when there are too many people and the jobs are ill defined, everyone believes somebody else will do the job. In fact less work gets done with more people. It is important that everybody has a full and challenging job to do. At the same time, it's essential to strike a reasonable balance. Not too much work and not too little.

Companies in a growth mode have a very difficult time getting the right amount of employees. They tend to either ride ahead of the growth curve or lag behind. Everybody wants to gear up for the coming onslaught of business. Nobody wants to be caught behind the eight ball. My experience was if we could run slightly behind the growth curve, people were more satisfied and it certainly worked better from a profitability standpoint. It is very important, however, not to get too far behind because you don't want your people stretched to the point of burnout. Admittedly, it's a balancing act.

Loyalty has to go both ways; it can't just be at the whim of the organization. I know this isn't a commonly held belief in American business, but I will believe it until my dying day. If the organization screws up, it's not an individual employee's fault. If the economy is bad, it's not an individual employee's fault. I think organizations have to reflect that in their thinking. Cut the expenses someplace else. I personally like the Japanese concept of employment for life as long as the employee performs their job in good faith.

These days you hear it all the time. A major company facing a financial downturn announces a layoff of 30,000 people and the stock price goes up. Well, if I'm a shareholder, I don't want to own a company like that. I wouldn't be proud of that. Analysts on Wall Street see it as a numbers game. Well, it's not just numbers, it's real people involved. Some jerk has hired too many of them.

Imagine having 30,000 too many employees! I'd be damned ashamed if that were my situation and I had to announce that. These are human beings we are talking about. Families are affected. Nobody even has the guts to tell them face-to-face. You just get a notice in your paycheck that you no longer work here. It's heartless. You end up with a load of employees that don't give a crap whether they stay or not.

It's important to instill the belief in your people that the company is going to be loyal to them. If they know you are going to do everything in your power to hang on to them even through tough times, it creates tremendous loyalty. They'll work their butts off to try to fix things and they won't be spending energy looking for another job.

Unless a degree of permanence is offered to your employees, they will always assume impermanence. They will always be looking for the next gig. If you look around, everybody's always looking to jump ship. If you create an organization where people feel like the company cares about them and is not going to lay them off at the first sign of a downturn, your people will become fiercely loyal. To me, employees are a company's biggest asset. I don't want to throw my heavy machinery out the window and I don't want to kick my employees out the door.

Chapter 15

A Corollary to The Peter Principle
Sometimes jobs outgrow people

Laurence J. Peter had what I consider an excellent theory about organizations. The Peter Principle states, *"In a hierarchically structured administration, people tend to be promoted up to their level of incompetence."* This is an unfortunate reality in big business.

In our society, the higher the level of management is, the greater the financial rewards and recognition. You don't typically get the same opportunity for money and prestige by being an outstanding "doer." This forces the average person to push hard to climb the ladder until they do indeed reach their level of incompetence.

Through my experience of growing large companies from the ground up, I developed what I call the Corollary to the Peter Principle, which states: *"Organizations eventually grow past individuals. A person, who is competent within one phase of a company's growth, while staying in the same exact job, can become incompetent as the company grows."*

At Record Bar, we arrived at this painful juncture several times. Managers, who had been quite instrumental in growing our company to the next level, would become wholly inadequate at managing the tasks required in the new phase. While some individuals were able to grow and adapt, others floundered miserably.

I would find myself in a conundrum when loyal employees who did a good job for us during a rapid growth phase of the company were suddenly poor performers. They were overwhelmed by the growing demands. They'd become incompetent, not by rising up the ranks; they'd become incompetent while staying in the same place.

When a company is in a rapid growth mode, you can't start retraining people. You just don't have the luxury of time. Once it was past them, it was past them. I found myself in the unsavory position of having to fire good people who had once been valuable contributors.

This confused people, particularly outside our organization, because there was this idea that had developed that we didn't fire people. It's true, I don't believe in laying off people, but I do believe in firing people when it is in the best interest of the organization. I believe strongly that if someone is doing their work, we owe them a job. Conversely, if we've given someone a job, they owe us effective performance. The idea that you should never fire anyone is just stupid. I don't want to haul a bunch of people around who aren't producing. It builds resentment among those who are working hard and doing their job.

Some people produce and some people don't. The ones that don't produce have to go. There is a real delineation between laying someone off for convenience and firing someone for cause. It was a real dilemma for me when people who had been good producers in the past, but could no longer produce as the company grew.

As I see it, there are three options when the demands of the organization outgrow the ability of an individual — two of which don't work for the organization and one that does. You can leave a person to flounder indefinitely in their job until the stress forces them to leave on their own. You can demote them, move them, or stick them in an office with no windows or telephone where they can do no harm. Or you can fire them.

I don't believe you can go backward with people, and I don't believe in demoting people. If you pull back their job description to meet their level of competence, you've got a problem because you are paying them for a bigger job. Whether you demote them with their pay intact or demote them with a cut in pay, they'll end up pissed off. Their dignity is hurt, their effectiveness is reduced, and they end up really unhappy. When people reach that level of incompetence in an organization, sooner or later, one way or another, they are going to leave.

I felt it was my duty and my responsibility to chose what was right for the organization rather than what the individual might prefer. I wanted to be the greatest guy in the world. I wanted to take care of our people, be the great father figure, but it didn't always work that way. I was paid to make the hard decisions.

A lot of times things happen in an organization through no particular fault of anybody. Rapid growth wields a two-edged sword. Some people just can't acclimate themselves to the new level that growth dictates. On those occasions when our growth outstripped the ability of individuals to manage, I found the only solution was to replace them with new people who were better suited to the organization.

When an employee becomes incompetent because the company's needs outgrow their capabilities, it is kinder to let them go. Whether they think so or not, I believe it is better for them to leave, to find a place that's a better fit, where they can be happy and comfortable in their jobs. Meanwhile, the company can get on with the business at hand without having to step around the casualties incurred through rapid growth.

Behind the Scenes with Barrie

The Celebrity Circuit
Hanging out in the fast lane

I had the privilege of visiting the White House four or five times when Jimmy Carter was in office. Carter had some music industry associations and often invited musicians for in-house concerts. Arlene and I were invited to most of them. I don't think it makes a lot of difference what your politics are, as an American, when you go through the front door of the White House, that's pretty exciting. It's an incredible experience.

I was so impressed with Jimmy Carter as a human being. He exuded a genuine warmth and intelligence and seemed sincerely interested in what you had to say. Too many politicians lack that kind of sincerity.

The first time Arlene and I met him, we were at a music industry trade convention where Carter was the keynote speaker. He had just taken the lead in the presidential race and it was a few weeks before the election. We went to a small cocktail party for the association's Board of Directors to meet with Jimmy Carter before his speech.

This was the 70's when Arlene and I used to smoke dope, and we made the mistake of smoking a joint before we went to the party. We were walking down the hall on our way to the cocktail party, when we saw all these guys talking into their lapels, you know, secret service agents. We were totally paranoid; we just knew we were going to get busted.

As we made our way into the cocktail party, we were having this surreal experience with all the paparazzi camera flashes going off everywhere. Then Carter came in and we were introduced to him. We started talking and he found out that we were from North Carolina so he asked Arlene, "Where are you from?" Well, Arlene was stoned, and she just nodded and said, "Yes, yes." So I nudged her and we blurted out, "Chapel Hill" and started laughing. Not our standard decorum.

As the cocktail party was ending, all the people with Carter were supposed to march into this large ballroom where he was going to make his speech. The guy in charge of the event decided to flip the lights on and off as a way of letting everyone know it was time to get seated. The Secret Service guys reacted as if there was a threat and went for their guns. We were stoned and already paranoid, so you can imagine what went through our minds. I was looking for a table to go under. We were scared to death, just totally freaked out! We crossed paths with Jimmy Carter a number of times, but this is my most vivid memory. Altered states and politics don't mix.

* * *

There was a period of my life where I got pretty heavily into the LA/New York party scene. Luckily I survived and went back to my normal life. I have fond memories of some of those parties. Some of the funniest things happened at our industry conventions. The record labels would bring in major acts to entertain us. It was their way of saying thank you to the retailers who sold the music, and to encourage us to sell even more. Typically after the act performed, there would be a cocktail party, so the key players in the industry could meet the entertainers.

These parties always started out for a very few people and ended up with a cast of thousands squeezed into a small hotel suite. It would be hot, smoky and full of people looking over your shoulder trying to see who else was there. Generally, it was not a lot of fun. Nevertheless, it was important for me to be there from a business standpoint.

We were invited to one of these parties when Motown Records was celebrating its 30th anniversary and Stevie Wonder was the featured performer. One of the marketing guys from Motown came up to Arlene and me and invited us to a small party in a suite for Stevie after the performance. There was no graceful way to turn it down. I pretty much had to go. I would have loved to meet Stevie Wonder and have a nice conversation with him, but not in that environment—we knew it would be a mob scene.

Arlene and I decided we'd go real early and try to get the hell out of there before the hordes of people arrived. When we got to the suite, there were only a few people there and Stevie had an absolutely drop dead gorgeous woman sitting on his lap. He couldn't see her, but he could certainly feel her presence.

As we walked into the room, the marketing guy came running up to us, and said, "Stevie can't wait to meet you!" I was thinking, "Stevie can't wait to get the hell out of here either?"

He brought Stevie over to greet us and we exchanged pleasantries. This was when Stevie was wearing his cornrows and braids with the beads hanging down. We got set for the obligatory photo, with three or four people in the picture. However, Stevie was facing the back of the room, while the rest of us were facing the front towards the camera. Obviously, Stevie didn't know where the camera was. Arlene, wanting to get the damn picture and get out of there, took Stevie by the shoulders and sort of whipped him around, sending the beads flying. I thought Stevie was going to get whiplash. It lightened the mood and we all had a good laugh. As we said our goodbyes and turned to leave, Stevie went back and resumed his position with the gorgeous woman on his lap.

* * *

I had another photo op at a party featuring a group called Supertramp. They had a popular album called Breakfast in America. On the cover of the album was a woman dressed as a waitress and holding a plate, with the band members standing on the plate. The woman holding the plate was an actress named Libby. She was a very large, amply endowed woman. I went to the party and Libby was taking pictures with people. Luckily or unluckily, I was the first person to take a picture with her.

I still have the picture. Unfortunately it's black and white, because you can't see that my face is beet red. My hair's all messed up and I'm sort of disheveled, because right before the picture snapped, she grabbed my head and shoved it right between her boobs. Photos with celebrities put more stress on the fan than it does on the celebrity, especially if there's a chance of being smothered to death.

* * *

Arlene and I were introduced to Roger Federer, perhaps the greatest tennis player of all time. We were at the tournament in Palm Springs, and a publicity person took us to the player's lounge to meet him. He was waiting for us. When we walked up to him, he graciously stuck out his had and said, "Hi, I'm Roger." I thought to myself, "No kidding."

He was warm and absolutely wonderful. He asked us questions about ourselves and seemed genuinely interested in who we were. I'll be a Federer fan for life.

* * *

Desmond Tutu spoke in Santa Barbara, and we went to a dinner in his honor. When we were introduced, I was surprised that he didn't take himself very seriously. He had a wry sense of humor, and I could see why people followed him. He was a delight.

* * *

Princess Grace of Monaco (a.k.a. Grace Kelly) gave a poetry reading on the Duke University campus. Afterwards, there was a reception, and we got to meet her. She was long past her movie star days and had put on a bit of weight, but there was an elegance and a presence about her that I've rarely encountered.

* * *

I've been able to sit on stage at concerts a few times, but one time the group Alabama got me on stage and presented me with a gold record for helping them. The energy that comes towards the stage from 10 or 15,000 people is amazing. I wasn't particularly frightened, but I sure wanted to get off that stage.

* * *

The coolest award I ever received was backstage at a Sting concert. Sting presented me with an award for helping sell a Christmas album that he had put together for children's charities. He told me that this was the first time he had ever presented anyone with an award because he was always on the receiving end. He thought it was very funny.

* * *

When the Eagles played in Raleigh, North Carolina, Irving Azoff, their manager, was kind enough to let us sit on stage. My daughter Janis brought her friend, whom we found out later, had never been to a concert.

After the show we spent time at the hotel with the Eagles. It was just us and the band, although the party for them was going on in a different room.

Joe Walsh was wearing one of the back stage wrist bands that only the Eagles wore. She asked him about it, and he gave it to her. It was the first time I ever wanted to steal something from one of my kids.

I always wanted to know what Janis' friend told her parents about that night, and if they believed her.

When it began . . . Arlene and Barrie dating in 1959

Johnny Cash after his performance at the University of
North Carolina 1964

Joan Baez at a Record Bar Convention

Jimmy Carter at a music industry cocktail party
in Miami 1976

Barrie's childhood hero Roy Rogers

George Jones and Tammy Wynette in Atlanta at
a Record Bar function

Barrie chatting with Joni Mitchell and Robbie
Robertson

Harry and Sandy Chapin at Carowinds in Charlotte,
North Carolina 1978

At their home in Hilton Head 1979

George Harrison at a Warner Brothers convention in Acapulco

Comedian, actor, and talk show host Howie Mandel

Dinner at Michael Jackson's house to preview
Michael's new album *Bad* 1987

Lyle Lovett in front of the Chapel Hill, North Carolina
Record Bar early in Lyle's career

Andrew Lloyd Webber at the opening party at the Metropolitan
Opera for *Phantom of the Opera* in New York 1988

Desmond Tutu in Santa Barbara 2005

Roger Federer at a tennis tournament in Palm Springs 2007

Part IV:

People Who Are Successful, Are Successful

Are Successful

Chapter 16

Don't Give It All at the Office
Having a life outside the workplace

We live in a culture that tends to reward the workaholic. I think that's just wrong. Many companies expect a dues paying period from their employees before they can get into the club. For example, bright, young, ambitious graduates come out of law school only to have the law firm just kill them during the first few years. They routinely expect 100+ hours a week. Law firms are not alone in this. Investment banks, Silicon Valley startups, and advertising agencies, just to name a few, act as if they expect your firstborn in exchange for a paycheck. The message is "those with a personal life need not apply."

The game becomes a sort of survival of the fittest, a weeding out mechanism to determine who's really dedicated to the work. I absolutely disagree with this methodology. I think many times companies weed out the wrong people. They run off people who have any expectation for balance in their lives.

At the end of a few years of giving it all at the office, people end up burned out and cynical as hell. There is some evidence that the mid-life crisis is occurring much earlier these days—often in men and women in their thirties. Career burnout is becoming an epidemic. Not only are companies losing bright and capable people, they are driving highly qualified people out of their industry entirely.

People who have enthusiasm and like what they do are priceless assets to any company. A churn and burn mentality creates high turnover. The costs of hiring, training, and losing valuable expertise are unacceptable in my book. I don't want anybody working for me 100 hours a week. That's not a talent that I'm interested in. I want somebody to take 40 or 50 hours a week and make them really quality hours. I believe in a concept of balance where you work hard and play hard.

My belief is that the worst thing you can do from a financial standpoint is to let a good employee get away. You lose all the experience and you lose good people. Give me a good solid employee, let me manage them for the long haul, and I will run rings around any company that burns out their people and tosses them aside in favor of younger, more energetic new hires.

Sometimes this workaholic culture gets carried to the extreme. If anyone should understand the negative impact of overwork, it ought to be the hospital industry. Yet med students, interns and nurses are routinely worked to the dropping point. When health professionals make mistakes, people die. Hospitals say they can't survive without making staff work long hours for low pay and ridiculous hours. I just don't agree. It's a far more expensive way to do business in the long run. These are disasters waiting to happen.

Recently, a friend of mine was the victim of a totally botched diagnosis in ER. She went to the hospital feeling extremely nauseous. She was diagnosed as having a kidney stone and sent home to pass it. They missed the fact that her MRI very plainly showed she had burst an ovarian cyst. They blew the diagnosis and she got really, really sick. The last thing I want when I'm really sick is somebody overly tired trying to diagnose what's wrong with me.

Now, I'm not in favor of the other extreme, like in France where a full-time work week is considered to be 30-35 hours. I don't think the solution is to work too few hours. To me the ideal is 40-45 hours a week, with a two to four week vacation, depending on seniority, spread out over the year—every year. I think people need time away from their jobs, particularly after they've been there for a while. It gives them balance and perspective in their life. People need to get away on a regular basis to clear away the cobwebs and to recharge their batteries.

There are of course times when you have to work some long hours to meet a deadline, avert a crisis, or raise a sinking ship. Certainly I would expect my people to step up to the plate and pull out all the stops under these circumstances. But I'm talking a few days, a few weeks or even a few months of long hours. There is never a justification to expect this kind of commitment from your employees day after day for years on end.

I'm looking for productivity in the long term; I'm not looking for productivity in only a five-year period. I want somebody who's going to be with me for 15-20 years and will still like coming to work every day. I don't want people who jump jobs every three or four years. I want to find good employees and keep them happy in the workplace. I believe happy people are the best workers. They're the ones who get the best results.

If you find yourself in a culture of workaholics, and you value having balance in your life, find somewhere else to work. There are organizations that understand the value of having a life outside of the workplace.

~

People who are successful are successful. You might think that sounds redundant, but hear me out. My experience of people in the workplace is that the truly successful role models are the people who demonstrate success not just in the workplace but also in their personal lives. I believe the best employee is a balanced employee. An individual that has a satisfying life outside of work has a better chance of becoming a long-term, productive employee.

The kind of people I always wanted to work for me had a keen sense of balance. They enjoyed their work, and they enjoyed their time away from work. When at work, they worked hard. When at play, they played hard and engaged in a variety of interesting activities. That's the kind of people I like to have around me, personally and professionally—people who lead full and diverse lives.

There is a tendency to admire the workaholic for all the good work and apparent dedication to the company. However, it's been my observation that inevitably their personal life goes to hell, and eventually their business life goes to hell too because they ultimately burn themselves out.

In the early days of running Record Bar, I created a "Martyr of the Week" award. The winner was often the one we'd hear saying, "I can't believe I work sooo hard!" It was a playful way to gently give someone a message to get a life. If you think you've got to work all day and all night, don't tell me about it; I don't want to hear it.

I remember this one guy in purchasing saying, "Man I was here until two o'clock in the morning," and I said, "What the hell are you doing?" I thought it was a form of insanity. Eventually he left because he felt unappreciated—everybody else wasn't making the same effort. I'm sorry, but martyrdom just doesn't impress me.

In my experience, a true workaholic is someone who is hiding out from his or her home life. They are so unhappy at home, they would rather find an excuse to stay at work all the time. I've tried talking to workaholics to gently point out that there are other things to do in the world besides working day and night. It's a tricky conversation. It's hard to tell somebody what he or she ought to do in their spare time, when you're already telling them what to do at work. When it was obvious that somebody didn't want to go home, I felt compelled to intervene. I found that approach to be totally unsuccessful. When people are deeply entrenched workaholics, they tend to have emotional and psychological issues way beyond what I can counsel. In the end, our culture drove out the workaholics. They weren't happy in the environment. They just didn't feel appreciated for their sacrifice. We placed a high demand on performance during working hours, and we encouraged people to go home at the end of the day.

When I hired people, I'd say, "Look. I usually go home at a decent hour, five or six o'clock. If you're still in your office when I go home, I'll feel guilty, so how about going home at a decent hour too?" My idea of productivity is to get more out of each hour, not to work all night long.

I'm unlike a lot of business people. To me the choice is obvious. If you have to choose between your business life and your personal life, I think personal life ought to come first every time. I think people who don't do that have a screwed up value system. It's more important to be at your kid's birthday party than to be at some business meeting. There has to be balance between your business life and your personal life. It's a juggling act for both men and women.

At Record Bar, we required people to take vacations—they had no choice; we wouldn't allow them to just accrue vacation time forever. People need to recharge. The company benefits from having well-rested, content, and happy folks around, and the individual benefits as well. It goes back to this, if people are relaxed and enjoying their lives, they are more productive. Well-rounded people bring more to the organization.

I always heard the buzz about people at work, and the prevailing belief was that you were either great at business or great at life. I'd hear them say someone was a great husband or wife, but didn't quite get it at work, or vice versa, they were great at the job, but couldn't make it work at home. That wasn't my observation at all. I firmly believe successful people are successful wherever they are.

People who are successful by my definition treat other people with respect and kindness. They are ethical and honest, and I just don't think you can do that in one place without doing it in another place. People who are ethical and honest, loving and caring, are like that all the time, not just some of the time. People who are truly successful are successful in work and play.

If you give it all at the office, you're not going to have much of a life. Give me your best work for 8 or 9 hours a day, then go home and hug your kids, kiss your spouse, walk the dog. Tomorrow's another day.

Chapter 17

Winners Win
Identifying the good people

I believe the best predictor of future behavior is past behavior. Someone who has screwed up in a previous job is probably going to screw up again. Past behavior usually repeats itself. Winners win.

Look at professional baseball or basketball. People who are publicly fired then get hired by another team because they want someone with experience rather than taking a chance on the unknown. It is the same in any industry. When people in the upper echelons of a leading company would get fired, a competing company would quickly hire them. They were coveted for their experience and were inevitably offered a better job than the one they had before. At Record Bar, we developed a name for it. We called it failing up.

Sure, once in a while someone who is genuinely good can get caught up in a bad situation in a company. There are always political reasons, abusive environments, or strategic circumstances that can create unfortunate ousters. But for every one of those, there are ten valid explanations that place the blame squarely on the individual.

People who succeed tend to succeed over and over. People who win tend to win again and again. After a while, I only wanted to interview people who had a successful track record.

The only problem with this is that when you look at it from the outside, some people who look successful aren't. They have become experts in the art of illusion and creating a positive spin. You have to get good at ferreting out the good ones. That means spending a great deal of time and attention on the process of interviewing and thoroughly checking references.

Interviewing people for a job is a real art. To do it well requires a lot of finesse. Nothing is more important than the hire. Hire the right person and you're in business. Hire the wrong person and you are screwed.

I don't believe in hiring by committee. Trying to gain consensus from the masses takes too long, it's unnecessary, and it's too hard on the candidate. I mean, how many people can you suck up to? The candidate ends up covering the same territory over and over, and nobody ever gets an in-depth view of the person. It is ultimately the manager's decision, and the manager needs to spend the time necessary to get past name, rank and serial number.

Asking the right questions, really listening to the answers and reading between the lines are essential skills in hiring. I like to conduct interviews in a relaxed, unhurried environment, giving people the space to do a lot of talking. I want to know about this individual as a person, not just about their job capabilities.

A good interview takes time. My interviews could take an hour or two. You've got to give a candidate time to reveal who they really are. It's as much about instinct as intellect. If I could get people to talk about their personal lives, what they liked and didn't like, I could ascertain a great deal about their character. General, open-ended conversation like this is a great way to get a real feel for someone.

This is tricky, because there are places you can't go, questions you can't legally ask. You have to be careful about what you ask someone, being sure to stay within the bounds of the EEOC regulations. What you can do is create a comfortable rapport and an ease of conversation that will invite a candidate to open up and veer from the script. I want more than just the facts. If I can sit down with somebody for a length of time, I can usually figure out the person behind the mask.

I pride myself on my instincts about people, but even I have been duped. People have a tendency to… how do you say…lie. Unfortunately I've had run-ins with the worst of the worst including sociopaths—really smooth individuals who can weave a web of lies so tight it's completely seamless to the naked eye. Always, always check references. It's amazing what you can learn when you ask the right questions.

Whenever possible, I have always conducted my own reference checks. In this day and age, people have to be so careful with what they say when giving a reference to avoid getting sued. Just as in the interview itself, you have to establish a rapport with the reference and try to get them to open up. Sometimes people will tell you straight up. Once again, instincts are crucial in helping you spot someone who is whitewashing the truth. As a rule of thumb, if a current boss is selling too hard, I figure they are trying to get rid of somebody.

The hire is the most important decision a manager makes in business. Investing significant time in the process of interviewing and really getting to know a candidate is time well spent. Trust your instincts, but verify by checking references carefully. You want a winner in business, not an award-winning actor.

Chapter 18

Customer Service Is an Art
Being nice to customers

I spent a good portion of my business career trying to get employees to be nice to customers. The retail record business operates with a thin profit margin, and it's an industry where everybody has the same music at close to the same price. If you want repeat business, you've got to make sure that your customers leave with the memory of a pleasant experience.

At Record Bar, our challenge was to differentiate our product by offering superior customer service. Sure, we could differentiate to some degree with location or inventory, but by far, it was our customer service that made Record Bar feel special. We made it our business to ensure that our customers had a great experience when they shopped with us.

The key to making that great experience happen is in the hire. In order to provide superior customer service, it's important to hire the right people – people who are friendly, approachable, and who will make the customer feel at home. It's easy to create an attractive environment and an enjoyable place to shop, but it's often the interaction between the customer and the salesperson that determines whether or not the customer comes back for more.

Typically, people who work in music stores are young and counterculture. They are usually introverted kids who would prefer to just sit at home and listen to their own music. They come off with an attitude that it's an imposition to have to interact with people—especially some old guy looking for Lawrence Welk. They are far more comfortable interacting with people exactly like themselves, with those that share the same values, the same taste in music, the same style of dress. Initially that's what we were dealing with at Record Bar, kids who were judgmental about music and not your ideal salesperson, visually or temperamentally. Change was not on their radar screen. They were unwilling to adapt to the sales environment and to suspend their judgment of others who were different from themselves.

Since Record Bar stores were located in high traffic malls, we were paying high rent to bring consumers by our door. Mall traffic tends to offer a mixed crowd including older consumers, not just hip teenagers. It became critically important to ensure we had a staff that would be tolerant of a diverse array of customers with a wide range of musical tastes.

It was obvious early on that we either had to hire different kinds of people, or we had to retrain the people we had. We realized we had been hiring the wrong kind of personalities. The retraining effort was challenging. It was a lot easier to hire the right kind of people and teach them about music than to try to fix personalities. We started hiring outgoing, extroverted, friendly and tolerant people. Then we trained them on the specifics of our business and our expectations for superior customer service.

We made a concerted effort to create an environment that was more inviting and comfortable to our customers. We asked our people to try not to appear so counter culture, to turn down the music, and to play music that had a wider appeal, at least in heavy traffic times. During low traffic hours, they could listen to whatever off-the-wall tunes that energized them. We asked them to dress in a less threatening manner. It was okay to wear jeans. They just had to be presentable ones, no fashionable holes in them and no revolutionary t-shirts.

Next we set about the task of sensitivity training. First of all, we said, you've got to be here anyway, why not be nice to customers? It's the Golden Rule in business, if you are nice to people, they'll be nice to you. It will make your job so much easier and keep the paychecks coming too. Secondly, we said, don't judge people. Musical taste is wide and varied and customers come in all shapes and sizes. Chances are they will like something you don't. Accept their choice. Their taste is just as valid as yours. The Mormon Tabernacle Choir may not be hip in your book, but it brings paying customers to our store.

We used to try to get our people to go to other stores in the mall and see how others interacted with customers. When we found exceptional people, we'd try to hire them. Unfortunately, they weren't that easy to find. It amazes me that good customer service is still more of an anomaly than the norm.

It should be an expectation, but as a society we've gotten used to lousy customer service. We are used to being waited on by crabby, apathetic people. We remark when the service is good, but we should remark when it's bad. Why should we accept insolent behavior? Why don't we call it as we see it? Do we think that nobody listens, nobody cares, and nothing will change?

We had Customer Satisfaction Cards which were stamped and addressed to me at our corporate office. Employees handed these cards out to our customers and asked them to evaluate their experience of customer service. I personally read every card that came in. We ran monthly and annual contests for the person who generated the most cards. It didn't matter whether they were good or bad. We assumed that someone would have to be insane to give bad service and then hand a customer a card that was going directly to the CEO of the company. The winners were recognized throughout the company and paid handsomely for their efforts.

Employees with an outstanding number of responses got a congratulatory phone call from me. I don't mean for this to sound egotistical, but I found it to be a big deal to an employee to be recognized and personally appreciated by the President and CEO of a company. Now you'd have to be an idiot to be rude to a customer and then turn around and ask for his feedback, right? The few that did, regretted it. Our goal wasn't to fire the malcontents; we just wanted to ensure customer service excellence and to identify any behaviors that needed attention.

Occasionally I would contact a customer to get a better understanding of a problem, which would often be followed by a gift certificate as a thank you and a request that we be given a second chance to redeem ourselves. I loved talking to our customers. I couldn't think of a better use of my time. They provided me with insights that I wouldn't otherwise have had an opportunity to hear.

Perhaps if more of us complained to management, the behavior would change. Who knows? It's certainly worth a try. Instead of taking our business elsewhere and casting our silent vote with our feet, we should voice our complaints.

For some people being nice is automatic, for others there needs to be a little prodding. Friendly and helpful people attract and hold on to repeat customers. Plain and simple: Treat others as you would like to be treated. Be nice to customers, and they'll be nice to you.

~

I've become a Four Seasons groupie. I've stayed in Four Seasons hotels all over the world and, without exception, I feel at home and genuinely welcome. I love it when I walk down the hall and a hotel employee smiles and says, "Hello, Mr. Bergman. Are you enjoying your stay?" Arlene and I always choose Four Seasons wherever we go because the service is so extraordinary.

With Four Seasons, you don't feel like you are in some amorphous chain. Every hotel is a representation of the local culture. When staying in Hawaii, you are immersed in all things Hawaiian. When in Paris, you get a Parisian experience. Wherever you are in the world, you are treated to the delights of the local culture.

It is obvious that a Four Seasons employee's first priority is to take "customer friendly" to a higher level by taking the time to interact with each guest to make him or her feel at home. It is a part of the Four Seasons culture. A conscious decision was made by management to provide this gracious environment. Anything less is unacceptable. The Four Seasons strives to be the kind of place where everybody knows your name and to create a warm and welcoming atmosphere. To me, that's what sets them apart. It can be duplicated anywhere. Anyone can do it. It's all about the commitment to do so.

Occasionally my travel adventures turn into misadventures. Recently, while I was staying at the Four Seasons in London I took a fall in the shower. The hotel staff was wonderful. They took care of me and got me to a hospital. It wasn't cataclysmic, but it was upsetting. The general manager was aware of my discomfort and communicated his concern to his staff. The Four Seasons' well trained staff is dedicated to providing a superior level of customer service, and I became the beneficiary. I got the royal treatment.

For several days after, I was a celebrity in the hotel. Everyone I encountered made a point to inquire about my injury and recovery. Two different executives in the hotel made sure I was okay on checkout. The general manager personally handled everything concerning my fall. Not only that, the hotel paid all of my medical expenses. Unbelievable.

The Four Seasons has an organized well-established system of communicating with their guests. It's second nature for them to be cordial. What takes their service to this superior level is how they manage something unforeseen like my accident. Although their communication system is still intact, the same script that is used to welcome and greet people is no longer appropriate. They were able to change the script so that they could convey their concern over my well being. The staff of the Four Seasons always seems to know what to say and how to say it. Nobody wants to be sick in a hotel a long way from home. But if it has to happen I recommend a Four Seasons Hotel!

Customer service is an art. When it's done well, which it rarely is in our country, the results are amazing. Good customer service creates fierce loyalty and an enthusiastic word-of-mouth. We met two women in Hawaii who made a game of staying at Four Seasons Hotels all over the world. It was fun to compare notes and share wonderful experiences with fellow groupies. They couldn't wait to book a vacation at the Four Seasons in Prague after we told them about our stay there.

In the memorable words from the theme song for *Cheers*, "Sometimes you wanna go where everybody knows your name." That's the hallmark of great customer service.

Behind the Scenes with Barrie

She's Got Bette Davis Eyes
Amazing elevator encounters and more

When you are in cities like Los Angeles or New York there are a lot of famous people around. I'm good at spotting celebrities. I think most people don't see them because they don't look or they don't care. I've always been a people watcher and I'm particularly fascinated by the antics of the stars. I guess I'm just a celebrity suck.

I've had some particularly interesting encounters with celebrities either while riding in an elevator or while waiting for one. Always the observer, I get a kick out of watching the strange and unexpected things people do when the camera is turned off.

I was waiting for an elevator at the Sherry-Netherlands Hotel in New York. While I was standing there with nothing else to do, I watched as a hotel employee walked past me with an armload of dry cleaning and knocked on the door of one of the big suites. I heard a woman's voice call out, "I'm coming." The door opened to reveal a tiny little woman less than five feet tall. I had to pick my jaw up off the floor when I recognized it was Bette Davis standing there with her hair in curlers and wearing footies. In a flash, her door closed, the elevator came and I got in and left. But that vision is indelibly etched in my brain. It was a truly astounding moment.

* * *

Another time, Arlene and I had just checked in at the Carlyle Hotel in New York. We were riding up in the elevator, and the elevator stopped on the third floor. It was not our floor, but without thinking we got off and turned the corner. The woman who was waiting for the elevator when we got off ran after us to tell us she didn't think we meant to get off there, pointing out that the only thing on that floor was the health club. The woman was Meg Ryan. What a nice and totally unexpected thing for a major Hollywood star to do. That forty-five second encounter told me so much about her character.

* * *

One day we were walking through the lobby at the Ritz-Carlton and noticed that Maria Shriver was there with her Dateline crew. Arlene was excited to see her there, since she had always been a big admirer. Later that night, we went out to dinner with a bunch of friends. After drinking quite a bit and raising some hell, we returned to the hotel and spotted Maria Shriver once again in the lobby. As we got in the elevator and the door closed, Arlene started yelling, "Did you see Maria Shriver? Did you see Maria Shriver!" Right then the elevator door opened and Maria was standing there laughing. She was so good-natured about it. Arlene was very embarrassed.

* * *

I met Howie Mandel at an industry party. He was quiet and shy and had very little to say. But I still found him friendly. I later saw him leave the party in a taxi, and I was surprised that he didn't leave in a limo.

* * *

We had dinner with Mary Tyler Moore. She was at Duke University generously helping aspiring actors. She was warm, gracious, and unassuming. After a while I forgot that I was talking to a legend.

* * *

Years ago, we got on an elevator for a long ride down to the lobby at a hotel in New York. As we stepped into the elevator we recognized the British actor, Albert Finney. He was standing there with a very attractive woman looking quite cozy. It was obvious that Albert had

had a great deal to drink. He started insulting me, for no particular reason I could tell. Perhaps he was just irritated about the interruption of their privacy. We had never met, but he continued to insult me all the way down to the lobby. We got out of the elevator and I haven't seen him since. What a bizarre encounter! Whether drunk or sober, people do the damnedest things in the confines of an elevator.

* * *

In my travels and through my associations in the entertainment industry, I met a lot of actors and actresses. Movie stars tend to be larger than life people because we carry around this whole Hollywood vision of them. And when you meet the real person, more often than not, they are nothing like what you expect.

One actor I met who was exactly like his Hollywood persona was Jimmy Stewart. I attended the Universal Studios release party for *The Glen Miller Story* and got to meet Jimmy Stewart and have my picture taken with him. He was exactly like he always was on screen—nice, warm and sincere. It's a wonderful moment when you get to meet a celebrity you've admired from afar and find they are exactly like you imagined they would be.

* * *

The celebrity I was most excited to meet was my childhood hero, the King of the Cowboys, Roy Rogers. We went to a small cocktail party in Beverly Hills for the release of one of his new records. We got there early because it meant so much to me to meet him. In fact we got there so early that the only people there were Roy, Dale, Arlene and me. We found out very quickly, that though he was a nice, pleasant man, he had very little to say. We had little in common, and it was difficult to carry on a conversation. Roy wasn't an overwhelming personality, but it was still a thrill to meet my childhood idol. It was one of the great moments of my life.

* * *

The last person I expected to meet at a cocktail party was Bob Dylan. Being a poet laureate of our generation, I expected he'd be spending his free time sitting up on a mountaintop chanting. I met him at a Columbia Records party in Beverly Hills. I talked to him for a long time. When he found out what I did, he was very interested in how his new record was going to sell. It became essentially a conversation about marketing. I kept thinking how extraordinary it was that this great poet, famous for writing "Blowing in the Wind", "The Times They Are A- Changin'" and "Like a Rolling Stone" was having a conversation about money and not his art. Look at his career and see how many times he's reinvented himself. I think he is brilliant.

* * *

I met Barbra Streisand at a convention. It was very atypical for her to attend such an event. She was scheduled to join us for a luncheon with just a few of the top retailers. While we were eating lunch, we saw her peek around the corner, but she didn't come in until everyone was finished eating. Though it was obvious that she was very shy, when she finally joined us, she was engaging and funny. She walked around and talked to everyone, posed for a group picture and left. I felt amongst the privileged few to get a chance to meet Barbra Streisand.

* * *

Many years ago, I went to a musical on Broadway called *Over Here,* starring the Andrews Sisters. The record company that created the sound track flew us up for opening night. They had a cast party at Sardi's, an old Broadway tradition. We met the Andrews Sisters and Abigail Van Buren, better known as columnist Dear Abby.

We were there for a while and I spent a good part of the evening talking to a young guy who was part of the chorus for the show. He was nineteen or twenty years old, a really nice kid, handsome, and very friendly. A year later, we saw that same kid in an insurance commercial on TV. I said to Arlene, "Look there's that guy I met at the cast party for *Over Here.*" A little while later this same kid became one of the stars in *Welcome Back, Kotter*—it was John Travolta.

So, keep your eyes open. You never know whom you might run into on the street, in a restaurant, or on an elevator.

Part V:

People Are The Best Game

Chapter 19

The Secret to Relationship Success
Learning to love and appreciate yourself

I've been married to the same woman for over forty years. It doesn't make me an expert about relationships, but it gives me some insight. We are happier now than we've ever been and we've been happy for a long time. My life is greatly enriched by my relationship with Arlene. We enjoy the hell out of each other's company. I'd rather be with Arlene than anyone else in the world—with the possible exception of Charlize Theron, but she hasn't called.

Happy people have good relationships. That means you've got to learn to love and appreciate yourself before you can truly love and appreciate another. It also means you've got to be keenly attuned to each others needs and make every effort to support your partner in pursing the things that will enrich his or her life.

When two people are together in a relationship, you have to learn to accommodate each other. Chances are I'm going to do some things she's not going to like, and she's going to do some things I'm not going to be crazy about either. It's hard to live with another human being if you expect them to behave as you would in every situation. Our charming idiosyncrasies can become sources of daily stress. Or, we can just learn to accept each other's way of being. The decision to accommodate requires asking yourself this question, "Is my relationship worth accommodating my partner, or would I rather be right?"

Accommodation can take many forms. It could be as small as deciding what movie we are going to see. For a relationship to work, you can't always have it your way at your partner's expense. Be sensitive to what is really important to your partner and go out of your way to ensure his or her needs are met. If every issue is going to become a battle, you are in the wrong relationship.

I accommodate Arlene because I love her. She accommodates me because she loves me. When we are at odds on an issue, we always sit down and listen to where each other is coming from and try to understand each other's feelings. Maybe that sounds like psychobabble, but it works.

One thing Arlene and I recognized a long time ago is that we couldn't find common ground regarding a sport we could enjoy together. I like tennis and she likes skiing. Instead of harping on each other about how much time we spend away from each other, we encourage each other to pursue what we love independently. That means I support Arlene going on ski trips and she encourages me to go play tennis several times a week. As a couple we've got a choice—whether we let it be a bone of contention or lovingly accept each other's interests. Supporting each other's happiness leads to relationship happiness and longevity. The space to pursue individual interests is very important in a successful relationship.

There is a fine line here. The premise of a healthy relationship is that, given the choice between being separate and being together, you pick being together. You each want some personal space, but for the most part, you'd rather be together. If couples are always heading off in different directions, living separate lives under the same roof, I assume they are in trouble. You've got to strike a balance between independence and togetherness.

It mystifies me when I hear guys today talking about the c-word: commitment. They say they are unable to commit to a relationship. To me, it's very simple. Unless you can commit to a relationship, you can't have one.

A relationship is a commitment by two people to adhere to a series of agreements. The problem with agreements is that unless they are explicit, they tend to be interpreted differently in the minds of the two people involved. Too often agreements are implicit—they are informal and open to interpretation. If you haven't sat down to discuss agreements, even for couples that have been together a long time, you will likely have different interpretations of the ground rules.

It's important to write down your agreements. Most couples have agreements about fidelity, economics, raising children and more. But even those kinds of things need to be spelled out in minute detail. These are the misunderstandings that land couples on a therapist's couch. Then the therapist will mediate the creation of agreements that should have been there in the first place.

Successful relationships are dynamic. It's important to recognize each other's strengths and weaknesses. One person is going to be stronger in some arenas than the other. For example, I suck at the management aspects of money, while Arlene's great at it. I'm pretty good at the financial overview part, so we meld our strengths together. As an entity we are far stronger than if the two of us were doing it separately. At different times, one person will be more dependent on the other depending on circumstances. It makes it interesting, one person's in charge for now, while the other person will be in charge later. It's balance of give and take that makes a relationship work.

Relationships only work if each person gives 100%. If only one person is giving 100%, you've got nothing. The idea of 50/50 is ridiculous. You can't be working half the time towards making it work. You've got to be in it all the way or not at all. It's like saying I'm going to be married on Monday, Wednesday and Friday—I'm taking off Tuesday, Thursday and Saturday. This is not kindergarten. It's hard work, but it's seriously rewarding. It's definitely worth the trouble.

I'm a strong proponent of marriage. I think that it's a good idea to live together first, to get an idea how it's going to work. I believe commitment is important. Saying I want to be with you for the rest of my life, then backing it up with a legal document has impact.

It confuses me why people care so much about whether people are the same sex, different sex, different religions, or different races. As long as two people want to be committed to each other, to love each other and care about each other's happiness, I think it's wonderful. I don't give a damn about controlling other people's choices. I think any loving relationship enriches the world around us.

I believe that personal relationships and business relationships are pretty much the same thing. When we think of relationships we always think about the romantic kind. Certainly these relationships are more intense, especially at first. After the initial excitement wanes, relationships between any two people tend to function in similar ways. That's why I believe if people are successful in their relationships in their home life they will be successful in their relationships in their business life.

Relationships can be created in odd ways and for strange reasons. I've always felt very close to Stevie Nicks, and I think she should feel close to me, because I saved her life in Mexico. We were at a Warner Bros. record convention in Puerta Vallarta and Montezuma's Revenge had made an appearance at the resort. I shared my diarrhea medicine with Stevie. To me that's as close as you can get!

Chapter 20

How We Present Ourselves
Observing human behavior

Watching people behave, or misbehave, is the best game I know. I can spend hours in an airport just watching what people do. Sometimes I play a game of making up stories about people, trying to guess what they do, where they are from, and what their belief systems are. Arlene and I will often entertain ourselves by making up stories about other customers in a restaurant.

I play the observation game in business as well. When I'm in a meeting, I've trained myself to observe details about other people. If I'm at the top of my game, I'll notice things like body language, breathing rapidity, tonality of speech, rapidity of speech, and eye movement. The better the quality of my watching, the higher my performance in a given situation. When you engage in conscious observation, people will give you extraordinary information about themselves, but you've got to look for it.

The observation game is part detective work and part intuition. No matter where I do it or whether or not I am accurate in my deductions, it makes me a better observer of human behavior. If I become a better observer of human behavior, I become a better manager. If I can figure out what makes people tick, I can figure out how to set up the conditions that enable people to feel empowered and motivated.

People have buttons, both positive and negative. If I can push the right buttons, and avoid pushing the wrong ones, they'll be happier, they'll work harder, and they'll be more successful—thus making me a happier person as well. If somebody has high control needs and I try to totally control them, we aren't going to get along. If they are like me and they start slowly in the morning, it's not a good idea to start telling jokes as soon as they come in the door. If I know somebody doesn't care much about sports, it's stupid to start a conversation about my favorite pro football team; they just won't hear what I'm saying and they'll turn off at the start of the conversation.

It is interesting to me that most people don't really look at other people. I've had people come up to me and say, "Hey Barrie, I really like your new beard!" I've had it for twenty years. Think about someone you saw this morning and try to remember what they were wearing or other details about how they looked. Were they happy and energetic, or angry and distracted? Most people are not very good at really noticing what's going on with other people. Most of us are too tied up with noticing what's going on with ourselves.

We present ourselves in a way that we want other people to see us. Even if we are sloppy in appearance, it's a study of sloppiness. We present ourselves in a way that we want other people to see us. Everybody does it. I spend time in the morning thinking about the way I'm dressing, the way I fix my hair, they way I look. My wife thinks I'm nuts when I wear a red t-shirt with orange shorts, but maybe it's because I just think they look good together.

Elevator behavior is a kick to watch. People reveal a lot about their character by how they behave in an enclosed space. Just watch what people are doing the next time you ride an elevator. I can tell a lot about people just from the way they push the buttons. If I go up to an elevator and I see that a button is lit and somebody is standing there, then there is no need to push the button again. But a fairly high percentage of people, who don't trust anybody else, will go push the button anyway. Some people on an elevator will stand there and look down the whole time so they don't have to make any human contact. This tells me that I'm dealing with a person who doesn't have a great deal of confidence.

I think it's great fun being on an elevator when it's full and then saying something totally outrageous just as I'm getting off. Like being on an elevator with a macho friend, and as the doors are opening for my floor, giving him a big kiss and saying the sex last night was great. The doors shut again and he's stuck on the elevator with a bunch of inquiring eyes.

I find it very interesting watching the way people create themselves. They tell us so much without ever uttering a word. If you look closely you'll find that they're telling you a bit about themselves. The message usually comes intuitively through their mannerisms, body language, and the way they talk with each other. This awareness of other people can be a valuable tool. When we are actively watching, we get a much better read about people. For me it's endlessly fascinating to watch what they do. And they do the damnedest things.

Chapter 21

Second Degree Unawareness
Not knowing what you don't know

Some people don't know what they don't know. I call this second-degree unawareness. People who don't know what they don't know are dangerous. If you are aware of what you don't know, you can either take steps to learn what you need to know, or partner with someone who has that expertise. However, if you are at the second degree, all you can do is plow ahead into the abyss.

I don't understand nuclear physics. I know that I don't understand nuclear physics. It empowers me because I know that I'm not going to try to explain, or delve into it. It stops me from making stupid mistakes. I know what I don't know.

There is nothing worse than dealing with a cocky S.O.B. that can't get past second-degree unawareness. They become very invested in creating the illusion that they know everything. They can't allow themselves to admit they don't know something, or that it's not an area of strength or expertise. They just don't get that they are creating more harm than good.

It is very difficult to talk to a person about a problem or an opportunity when they have no comprehension that there is a problem or an opportunity. It seems to be a trait of the young. As you get older you come face to face with your limitations, if you are smart.

Knowing what you don't know or what you can't do, or what you don't do well is important. People have limitations—physically, emotionally, and intellectually. I think recognizing those limitations and channeling your energy into developing your natural talents and skills is wise and empowering. This gets you moving in the direction where you will have the greatest probability of success

When you understand what your limitations are, you stay within the parameters of your own expertise. I often hear it said, "You can do anything you want if you work hard enough at it." I just don't believe that. I don't think that everybody should do everything. Some people are just naturally better at one thing than another. Having an organizational structure that works means having people that are good in different areas. There is synergy in that.

Managers do well to take advantage of a person's strengths and not try to force a bad fit. Don't take a data processing person and make them a marketing person. There is a pervasive belief that "You wouldn't want a manager who can't do every job." Of course I would! As CEO, all the people who worked for me could do their individual job better than I could, except maybe for sales because that was my strength. If you are a CEO who is better than your people in accounting, what the hell are you doing being the CEO?

The most bewildering people are those that are talented in too many areas—it confuses them. They jump around from place to place rather than concentrating or focusing in one area and excelling. I found it so frustrating because these people were so talented, but they could not focus. I was envious of their talent, but it made me crazy. You have to pick something as your focus, be the best you can be and let go of the rest.

Organizations have natural strengths as well. When you find one of those strengths it's important to keep your focus on that strength. When I was in the music business, we worked to clearly define what our business was. How wide was the arc? Were we selling music, entertainment, or were we just a hole in the mall that sold things? We decided we were selling pre-recorded home entertainment. Every time we dabbled in something outside our area of strength and expertise, we got in trouble.

You can't be all things to all people. Organizations and individuals have to make those decisions. Knowing what you can't do well is a great step forward. Understanding what our strengths are means also understanding and acknowledging our limitations. I don't think there is anything wrong with limitations—we all have them. If we can all capitalize on our individual skills and talents and work toward a common goal, that's how we all win. It works in sports, it works in business, and it works everywhere.

Chapter 22

One Person Can Make a Difference
The face of Bare Escentuals

After selling Record Bar and after a brief attempt at running a record label, I decided at forty-eight years old to retire to a life of leisure. That lasted for about a year. I had become friends with a guy named John Hansen when he was working for General Atlantic, a company that had an investment in Record Bar. While I was trying to figure out what to do with myself in retirement, John approached me with an idea he had for doing something entrepreneurial. I agreed to partner with him and invest in a new venture.

John wanted to do something in the Bay area, and he looked for anything promising. He found Bare Escentuals, a Body Shop knockoff. It was in bankruptcy.

When he told me that the cost of goods in cosmetics was 28%, I was hooked. The cost of goods in the record business was 62%, so I figured if we could sell any of this stuff, we could make some money and have some fun.

I thought that John already knew the financial side of the business, and I could help him with the marketing and operational sides. I believed that products can be sold by anybody, but I found out that it's not that easy. Thank God, we found Leslie Blodgett.

The company consisted of four retail stores selling natural cosmetics. We bought the company out of bankruptcy, closed two of the stores and re-capitalized the company. John set about learning how to sell cosmetics and took the helm as the CEO and Chairman of the Board. I offered my expertise in retail chain management and sat on the Board of Directors.

Five or six years into our deal, John decided to accept an opportunity to run a publicly listed company in San Diego, leaving us with the challenge of finding a new CEO for Bare Escentuals. At the time, the company was just rocking along, not experiencing extraordinary growth, but it was operating as a successful business. We didn't really want to invest the money necessary to recruit a CEO from the outside, so we decided to promote from within.

About a year earlier, we had hired a top-notch cosmetics merchandiser from Neutrogena. Leslie Blodgett had grown up in the cosmetics business. Her first job had been selling cosmetics behind the counter at Bloomies on Long Island when she was a kid. She understood that selling cosmetics was about selling the sizzle. It is a uniquely challenging business and it must be done with a very artful hand.

It turned out Leslie was and is a genius. She was a whirlwind from the start. She came in and changed our entire product line and got us into the mineral makeup business. She had been a brand manager previously, but had no operational experience running a business. Nevertheless, Leslie showed great promise and we felt that with our combined experience, we could mentor her in the skills she needed to run the company. She was very concerned at first that she wasn't up to the job, but John and I believed she could do it and we gave the CEO title to Leslie. Sometimes the person you're looking for is right under your nose. You just have to look.

What happened over the next four or five years was the most amazing explosion of a company that I have ever seen. It proved my theory that organizations run top down and that one person by the sheer will of their talent and determination can make a company successful.

One day, Leslie called me and said she'd been having trouble sleeping at night and was staying up late watching QVC, the TV shopping channel. She said, and I remember these words clearly, "I can do that!" Showing what a clever guy I was, I said, "Why would you want to? QVC doesn't sell much." She very quickly proved me wrong.

Leslie took our products, particularly Bare Minerals, and personally appeared on QVC to sell our products. The products were a smash hit from the first appearance and the product line remains a stunning success. She has the charm, know-how and salesmanship to convince women all over the world to buy these products. Year after year she sells more and more merchandise on QVC. The numbers are astronomical.

Leslie made all of the decisions about what to sell and how to market it. She went on QVC and used her personal charm and belief in the product to create a mass market. She turned the shows into a make-up party, and women all over the county responded to it.

A few years after Bare Escentuals became a household name on QVC, I had another memorable phone call from Leslie and yet another chance to prove my incredible business acumen. The conversation went something like this: "We should do an infomercial." I replied, "Why would you want to do that? Infomercials don't sell anything." Millions and millions and millions of dollars later, I've become a believer in the infomercial. Listening to the ideas of others, no matter how bizarre they may seem, can lead to great successes.

We tried to get a celebrity host. For various reasons none of them worked. We thought we had Leeza Gibbons, but at the last minute she changed her mind and started her own make-up line that was *very* similar to our Bare Minerals. (hmmm. . .)

Finally Leslie said, "I don't need a celebrity. I can do it myself." She also decided to use regular women, instead of models for makeovers. Every decision she made was a home run.

Bare Escentuals worked because John brought his talents to the table, I brought mine, and Leslie was a genius. We all were able to control our egos to make a cohesive team. This is how success is achieved.

Leslie is one of the most creative people I've ever met. It was so much fun to watch her do her thing. Her mind works like an artist— the way she comes up with names and product designations is like watching someone make music or create a painting. When you have a key contributor who has an artistic temperament, it's best to leave them alone and let them create. What seems like a strange or even wacko idea in the moment can grow into something huge when you've got a creative visionary at the helm. After awhile, I started saying to Leslie, "Don't even tell me, just go do it!"

Ironically, men run most of the cosmetic companies in this country. It makes a lot of sense to have a woman run a cosmetics business. Though Leslie did not have the type of resume you'd traditionally require of a CEO candidate, it was a gamble that paid off magnificently. We helped her understand how to run an organization, how to manage people, and how to find the key players that make an organization run. Leslie was so energetic and driven that she had a tendency to try to do everything by herself. After she took charge, the company grew so quickly and sales ramped up so fast she had to learn to delegate. She now has a great management team in place to run things so she can spend all her time doing what she does so well—generating sales and being Leslie Blodgett, the face of Bare Escentuals.

In 2004, we sold Bare Escentuals to Berkshire Associates in Boston for over 200 million dollars. I am grateful to John and Leslie for the vision and creative genius that created this incredible success story. One person *can* make a difference.

Chapter 23

One Person Can Cause a Disaster
Identifying the bad apple

As I've said before, I believe that organizations function in a pyramidal form. As long as you hire good people down the pyramid, good people beget good people. It is also true that if you hire one unethical person in a position of power and influence, everyone down the pyramid can become compromised. One person can take an organization and lead its people straight into a brick wall.

One of my executives at Record Bar was absolutely the most charismatic leader that I ever employed. He was a large guy, very handsome, extremely articulate, and really charming. He had charisma dripping from his pores. He had the ability to lead and to get people to follow. Unfortunately, he was also a pathological liar able to weave elaborate stories with virtually no regard for the truth. He was so good at it, that his lies went undiscovered for years.

He worked his way up through the company, starting as a clerk in one of our stores and ultimately becoming a senior executive. He was a stellar performer at every level. How much of that perceived performance was based on total crap, I can't say. He had me completely charmed—and completely fooled. He was a fun guy to hang out with. I would socialize with him outside of work, and even considered him a personal friend. For a long time, he had me snared in his web of deception.

His ability to lead was extraordinary. He did such a great job of developing loyal followership, that his people became virtual cult members. As a result, when things started to unravel, I had to cut away an entire layer of management beneath him. His people just couldn't believe that what this guy had been telling them wasn't the truth. There was no way in the world that I could convince these people otherwise. It was one of the saddest moments in my business career when I had to let them all go. These people had started out as excellent employees, but they had been led to engage in improper behavior by a manipulative master of deception.

If you are smart enough and charismatic enough, people will believe what you say. This guy told me things that caused me to act in certain ways toward certain people. I later learned that what he told me was absolutely false. Taking him at his word caused me to make some business mistakes and to act like a moron. He told me people said things about me that they didn't say. He told people I said things I didn't say. Unless a number of people start to compare notes, lies like this will go unchallenged.

It took time to discover his deception, but as most people who are cavalier with the truth eventually find out, the lies start to compound. After awhile, enough people told me different stories about the same event that his façade started to crack. I began to worry, but I still had no way to prove his duplicity. Then one day, a closely trusted employee of his ratted him out. The employee had been fired. She wrote a letter and said if you look here, you'll find this, and if you look there, you'll find that. These were very serious allegations of illegal and unethical behavior. I looked and I found. That's when I learned the magnitude of the problem

I'm the kind of person that tends to believe everything a person says, until I don't. When I have reason to stop believing, I get paranoid and I start examining everything. If people behave badly in one place, you can bet they are behaving badly elsewhere. Once you yank on the right thread, the whole thing comes unraveled. Nothing happens in a vacuum. Look deep and then look deeper.

What I discovered was irrefutable evidence of financial malfeasance. He had his employees behaving inappropriately—telling them that their actions were approved or sanctioned by higher ups, including me. Once I discovered the truth, it took about 15 minutes for me to fire him. His ethics violated everything I believed in.

In an ethical organization there can be no violation of the ethical base. Once an aberration is identified it has to be rectified. There can be no acceptance of unethical behavior. Even though it might be uncomfortable in the moment, organizations have to act immediately to remedy the situation. There are always mitigating circumstances—timing, personal relationships, or concern about negative impact on the business. There can be all sorts of arguments for turning a blind eye in the moment, so as not to rock the boat. In this case, I had his manager saying, "Let's not do this, it's not the time." I said, "I don't give a damn—this is not going to exist in my company!" I fired him and I fired five or six upper level managers who had been tainted as well.

One bad hiring decision cost us millions of dollars and ruined a lot of people's careers. The firings were uncomfortable, yet necessary. The wonderful part is that by doing the right thing, we came out the other side with our integrity intact and our profits restored.

Be careful who you hire and keep your eyes open. As a manager, be wary if things seem too good, because that just might be the case. This guy was great at painting rosy pictures. He was a font of good news. With him, everything was wonderful. When people are telling you all is well, you really want to believe it. Having a healthy dose of skepticism, and the use of a good microscope to illuminate what is not visible to the naked eye, is a very good idea. What you see is not always what you get.

Behind the Scenes with Barrie

Close Encounters of the Personal Kind
Experiencing celebrities without paparazzi

When my wife Arlene and I were dating in high school, we used to go to the Durham Armory to the all-black dances. Durham was on what was known as the "Chitlin Circuit"—a series of small to medium size towns in the South frequented by the great black rhythm and blues performers. This was in the mid 50s to late 60s and it was called "race music" at the time. The venues weren't great places to play, usually National Guard armories, but the dances would attract thousands of jubilant black people and a rare handful of white people. Arlene and I were always there.

At the time, North Carolina, like so many states in the South, had a law that you couldn't integrate a dance floor. These dances were for black people only and white people were relegated to the balcony. They'd have around 2000 people on the dance floor and maybe 10-20 white people in the balcony. It was a total juxtaposition. Arlene and I weren't allowed to go on the dance floor, but we could watch from the balcony. I got a small taste of what it must have felt like to be forced to the back of the bus.

Looking back, it's amazing, the people I got to see up close when I was just a teen: Fats Domino, Ray Charles, James Brown, Ike and Tina Turner, Jimmy Reed, Chuck Berry, all the great R&B performers. They were extremely accessible. After their music set, they'd go out in the audience and dance. There was not the kind of separation you get with rock stars today, so we got a close up view of many of these stars. To a young white kid who was just transfixed by the music, it was magical, just magical.

Even though we were restricted to the balcony while the dance was going on, I did get special treatment because I worked at my uncle's record store. We sold tickets to the dances and I got to know the promoters. I got to go back stage and into the dressing rooms to meet and get to know the performers. They thought it was neat that a white kid liked their music.

At one of these dances one night I got to meet the hottest act in the country, Sam Cooke ("Chain Gang" and many other hits). His music was just on the verge of crossing over to white audiences. I'm back in the little dressing room, sitting there talking to this guy who was suddenly one of the biggest stars in the country. He was just wonderful. I mentioned to him that my girlfriend was sitting in the balcony. He said, "Let's go meet her. How about introducing me?" So here I come up to the balcony with Sam Cooke so he could meet Arlene. I was just a kid and it was the coolest way ever to impress your girlfriend.

* * *

We also got to know James Brown pretty well. He played Durham a lot. James Brown is absolutely the most exciting black performer I've ever seen in my life. He really knew how to stage a show! They called him the "hardest working man in show business." He was a great singer, an incredible dancer, and he had a tremendous dramatic flair on stage. At the end of his act, he'd be just totally exhausted. He'd look like he was going to fall down in a heap. He'd be down on one knee breathing hard, then a guy would come on stage and put this cape around him and start to lead him off stage. He'd get just to the edge of the stage, when James would tear the cape off and come running back and start singing some more.

James would repeat this act 4 or 5 times. He would say, "I just can't do it anymore, I can't do it anymore," then whip off the cape and come running back on stage. Each time he would get more dramatic and the crowd would get wilder and wilder. Everyone was whipped into a frenzy. I've never seen anything like it.

We tried to see him anytime we could. He was just an incredibly flamboyant character. Every once and a while, at our store, the phone would ring, I'd pick it up and it'd be James. He'd ask, "How are my records selling?" You can't do any better PR than that.

James wouldn't go onstage anywhere until he was paid upfront in cash. He was a smart guy. Nobody was going to screw with him. At the time, a lot of performers were getting screwed by greedy promoters. James got smart and made sure he got paid. We were standing out in front of the Durham Armory while the promoter tried to collect enough money to get James to perform. We started chatting with the promoter and he asked us if we wanted to meet James. Of course we said yes. So he brought James out to meet us. We had this great conversation for a while. He said to us, "Are you going to the dance?" When we said yes, James took out the most gigantic wad of money I've ever seen. He peeled off two 100-dollar bills, gave it to the guy at the gate and said, "Here, let my friends come in." It was just the best!

* * *

The most exciting female performer at the time was Tina Turner, particularly when she was still working with Ike. She was an amazing dancer. When they had the Ike and Tina Turner Review with the Ikettes, it was really something to watch. I learned early on that she and Ike didn't get along—they hardly spoke to each other. Of course we know now that Ike was abusing her, but I didn't know it at the time.

I got to go backstage and was introduced to Tina along with Ben E. King in her dressing room. They were passing around a mason jar of bootleg white lightning and they let me taste the liquor. It was a moment of sheer joy for me. I was maybe 16 years old—it just doesn't get any better than that for a kid. I'm standing there with these two great entertainers, and they let me have some of what they were drinking. They were Gods to me. Alcohol can occasionally bring clarity.

Arlene and I used to go to a lot of other black clubs. Most of the time we'd be the only white people there, among hundreds or thousands of black people. Unfortunately, that came to a stop in the late 60s after the advent of the black power and black separatism movement and we weren't welcome anymore. Times change, and we must change and adapt to the times. What was acceptable at one point in time was no longer acceptable. It was sad, because to this day, I love the music. As Steve Martin has said "I was born a poor black child." Well, if you believe in past lives, I just might have been. The music is in my soul.

* * *

I love Bruce Springsteen. He's the best live act I've ever seen. I've never met him, but we did see him play at the 1972 CBS convention, when he was unknown. Bruce was dressed in black and Clarence Clemons was dressed in white, wearing a big pimp hat. Bruce was so exciting, we knew we had seen the future of Rock n' Roll.

He was supposed to play for 30 minutes, but he played for an hour and a half. All of the old CBS guys around us were bitching and moaning that the guy was playing too long and to get him off the stage. We thought we had seen God.

Years later we were invited to USA for Africa, where "We Are the World," produced by Quincy Jones, was recorded. It was a star studded night with everyone in Rock n' Roll performing.

The performance was held at the A & M Records lot. Guests were in black tie, giving an even more gala feel to the event. Christie Brinkley went around handing out fliers. Harry Belafonte and Sidney Poitier were there among the many guest celebrities.

When we first drove up and saw all the limos, we noticed a single figure getting out of a rental car across the street. It was Bruce. He had no entourage, no limo, just himself. Pretty cool, huh?

* * *

We were in the Bahamas for a CBS record convention, when Clive Davis was president of CBS Music. Clive had a small cocktail party in his bungalow and invited us. When we came in Clive greeted us warmly. I noticed that seated on a couch was Miles Davis.

Miles was one of my heroes. Clive took us over to meet Miles. As we were approaching from behind, he never looked around, he never looked up, he just stuck his hand out in back of him and muttered something. I knew his reputation as difficult, so I didn't take it personally.

* * *

We had dinner with Bonnie Raitt in New Orleans just before her huge comeback album was released. We had been chatting about Hilton Head, where Arlene and I had a house, and Bonnie had told me how much she and the guys in her band love the island.

I had heard the CD, and I told her how much I liked it and that I thought it would be the biggest seller of her career. She said, "I'll do anything to help it sell, but give Hilton head." Funny lady.

* * *

I spent several hours with the Rolling Stones backstage on one of their early American tours. Mick was charming and full of risqué stories about women, and Brian Jones and Charlie Watts were very friendly. Brian Jones was into American country music, which surprised me greatly. The entire time I was with the Stones, Keith Richards and Bill Wyman played blues riffs on their guitars. My impression has always been that British bands were a lot less crazy than American bands. These guys were very cool and oddly enough quite normal.

Part VI:

Three Singles and a GrandSlam

Chapter 24

Organizational Inertia
Dealing with organizational fear

A huge problem impacting growth in American business today is organizational inertia. Organizational inertia occurs when a culture of fear permeates the business, starting at the top and running down through all levels of the organization. When organizations become risk-averse, innovation is stifled.

Organizational inertia manifests when people are afraid to make decisions. At its very worst they are afraid to do anything at all. Individuals begin to adopt a survival attitude, believing that the way to keep their job is to never take a chance, to never do anything outside the norm.

A friend of mine told me about a major Hollywood studio that doesn't make movies anymore because everybody's afraid to give a green light. They have endless opportunities to secure first-look deals with A-list writers, actors, directors and producers, but nothing ever happens.

When an organization creates an environment of fear, you can take very capable, creative people and turn them into ineffective paper pushers. They come to believe the worst thing they can do is to make a decision. They don't want to risk being responsible for a project that could fail.

I believe that decisions in an organization should be made at the lowest level possible, and people should be empowered to make those decisions. At Record Bar, we said to people, "Nobody gets fired for making a bad decision; you only get fired for *not* making a decision." We wanted to get our people to move forward and take action, not sit on their hands and wait for permission.

People want to achieve. They want to act on creative ideas and make things happen, but you have to let them make mistakes. Intelligent people will learn from the experience and not make the same mistake again. If you're going to cut somebody's head off the first time they make an error, they aren't going to take risks. They'll stop trying, they'll never learn and they'll never innovate.

If you graph it, most organizations make progress by fits and starts. Over time, the graph will show a steady upward trend. The fits and starts represent a learning curve. In a culture of fear, that graph will flat-line in a hurry. I believe most competent people will make the right decision 90% of the time. If you just empower people to act, most of the time, they'll get it right. Unfortunately in this country, the larger the company is, the greater the bureaucracy. People become set in their ways, and innovation stops happening because bureaucratic organizations reward the status quo.

Look at the car manufacturers in Detroit. Twenty years ago, all the Big Three cars started to look alike. It bored the American public and consumers started to buy foreign cars that were cheaper and got better gas mileage. As foreign car designs became more innovative, there were fewer Americans willing to buy from Detroit. Eventually,

American car companies were forced to try some innovative ideas. Chrysler introduced the Prowler and the PT Cruiser. Ford began offering the retro Thunderbird and Mustang. They started to think outside that decades-old box. Instead of stamping out the same old car, which was the safe way to go and stifling to the company's growth, they began to take some risks. This change in direction brought the American buyer back home.

If a company has product that is doing well, not taking any chances or risks can be a very good short-term style. But staying with that strategy over the long-term is a recipe for disaster. It can be a huge mistake, if you don't keep an eye open to innovation and just keep on making the same widget over and over again. Eventually the competition will leapfrog over you. Sooner or later, you'll turn into a dinosaur. You can turn into a Sears. Here's a perfect example of a company that did not innovate. They did exactly the same thing for decades. And then the light bulb came on: they decided to sell brand name merchandise but they were 15-20 years behind.

Organizational inertia in some arenas is met with swift repercussions; you don't have the luxury of a decade or two to figure things out. The high tech industry is all about innovation, change and risk-taking. In this business if you snooze you lose. When Steve Jobs left Apple, we watched the company vegetate. When he came back, the company came alive. Look at the Ipod. Look at an *idea* like the Ipod. There is a spirit of innovation at Apple. It starts with Steve and permeates the organization. When Steve is around, people are energized. He turned the faucet back on.

You don't get that kind of dramatic innovation without somebody at the top saying its okay to fail. If the person at the top is only worried about next quarter's earnings per share, innovation isn't going to happen. CEOs become afraid of their boards and afraid of their own shareholders if, God forbid, their profits go down for a quarter. You've got to be willing to take chances and risk making some big mistakes if you are going to win big.

Risk-taking is the hallmark of the smaller, more nimble companies. Just look at Pixar. They created a whole new genre of wonderful animated film. Now that's innovation that didn't fall on the cutting room floor.

Chapter 25

The Theory of Hanging Around
Do what you do, and keep doing it

I've been doing some consulting. Consulting is an interesting job. I come up with wonderful ideas and my clients totally ignore me. It's great for my ego.

When I consult, I only do it with CEOs who are running companies that are on the way up. It's fun for me and I enjoy helping them so they don't have to reinvent the wheel. Occasionally, they do listen to me and save themselves some time and a lot of grief. It's not because I'm smarter than they are, it's because I'm older and more experienced. So many of the issues and problems they face are ones I've dealt with a time or two.

One issue that comes up repeatedly with my clients is focus. I'm convinced that the younger people are, the harder it is to focus. We live in an A.D.D. world that inundates us with images, sounds and experiences quicker than we can take it all in. In a society that's been brought up on MTV, we have less and less of an attention span, making it more and more difficult to focus. Coupled with impatience, this leads to a tendency for people to flit from one business model to another, never giving sufficient time or attention to one area long enough to reap the rewards.

In business, focus is paramount. The phrase I use all the time is "Do What You Do." Do what you do, do it well, and do it over and over and over. It applies to organizations and it applies to the individuals within organizations. I believe in the Theory of Hanging Around. If you hang around long enough, doing what you do, eventually an opportunity will show up. But if you don't hang around, it will show up and you won't be there!

As a culture, we've all been seduced by the idea of the overnight success. Everyone is looking for instant gratification, the easy path to wealth and riches. People forget that the dotcom phenomena turned into the dotbomb fiasco. You can't go from point A directly to point D. You've got to plod through the steps, first A, then B, then C and then you get to arrive at D. Success in business takes time, energy and hard work. There aren't any shortcuts.

Personally, I've never met a real overnight success. I've met people who've done something well for a long time and then got discovered. Then everyone assumes they came out of nowhere. It takes a long time to be an overnight success. It took 25 years to build Record Bar into the success that made me a wealthy man. Bare Escentuals was an overnight success after only 14 years. One thing both of these success stories have in common is time. The business models for the two companies were very different, but we achieved the same level of success, by hanging around for the long run, by showing up everyday to do our jobs, and by focusing on doing what we did and doing it very well. It's like three singles and a grand slam. Small successes over time lead to the big win.

Sitting here talking about focus and staying the course seems very simple. But on a day-to-day basis, it's hard to keep an organization focused. Entrepreneurial types tend to be creative, innovative thinkers.

Once an idea is launched, it's much more fun and intriguing to move on to the next great idea than to stick around to fully implement the original plan.

Let me tell you a tale of two clients of mine. Client A is extremely creative and talented. He came to me with a good business model that played to his strengths. Unfortunately, being the creative, A.D.D. type, he is absolutely incapable of focusing on his core business and doing that well. He's got an idea a minute. He just bounces all over the place. He comes up with these wonderful ideas, but they aren't related to what he is doing at any point in time, so he veers off in a new direction. That's a recipe for disaster. You've only got so much time, so much energy, so much money, and so many people. He chews them up and spits them out. The guy makes me crazy. Since I've been working with him, he has gone through one business model after another. Each one is the new thing that's going to be the home run. His business is struggling, and has been for years now.

Client B is also full of good ideas and has a good business model. He's had numerous opportunities to move away from his core business, and I've advised him against it. He is very good at focusing and executing his core business. He's a great leader and gets his people to focus their talent as well. It's not the most exciting business in the world, but it's damn profitable. His people like working for the company, they are excited about what they do and the company is growing at a fast pace, just booming.

Client A and Client B are equally talented, intelligent people. Both are entrepreneurs who started with nothing but great ideas. One is fabulously successful. The other is floundering and failing. The difference is focus and the commitment to hang around to see ideas through to fruition.

There's real nobility in doing something well. And when you hang around long enough, doing what you love and doing it well, chances are that in time something magical will occur.

Chapter 26

Boy Was I Dumb, and Boy Did I Get Smart
How I almost bankrupted my company

I've never been diagnosed with A.D.D., but at different times in my career my attention span has not been exemplary. I can become easily bored. Occasionally, when things were going very well at Record Bar, I became restless and started to tinker with the company. A friend of mine often said that I would fuck things up just so I could fix them, but I always denied that. He may have been right.

Two different times, I brought in outside consultants and gave them a position of authority in the company. Consultants like to stir things up. The consultant style is to come in with a flurry of activity and create a lot of change very quickly. With a company that's in trouble, this can be a good shock treatment. But for a company that is doing well, it's the fastest way to screw it up that I can think of. It makes people insecure and outright frightened. I learned the hard way that a consultant's style is not a good style for ongoing operational leadership.

The first time I brought in a consultant as an employee, I made him our Chief Operating Officer. This was a gigantic mistake. One would think I would have learned from this experience, but it took me two inoculations to get the picture. Ten years later, I hired another high-powered consultant to run the company for me. I turned over the reins as CEO and faded into the background, while he proceeded to make a series of colossal mistakes. He damn near took us out of business while I sat there and watched.

The biggest mistake made by our newly anointed CEO was to lose sight of our business model. We were a retail music company. He expanded the company into the wholesale video business. Suddenly, we were dealing with a whole new kind of customer, some of whom were our retail competitors. The best thing about the video rental business was the cash flow, but that was not the case on the wholesale end of the business. Our receivables got totally out of hand. The negative cash flow for our video wholesaling created such a drastic cash flow shortfall for our retail record stores that it nearly put us out of business. Key business insight: Buy low, sell high.

My rocket scientist CEO, the former consultant, decided that to improve our cash flow, we would cut our inventory in our stores, which (surprise) caused our sales to go down. Then in a bold stroke, he cut our inventory again, which, of course, caused our sales to plummet further. Dumb, dumb, and dumber.

We went from a company with a very high IQ to a very stupid company at warp speed. It pains me to talk about this, because I was the lead clown in this story. Although I wasn't the CEO, I was the Chairman of the Board and I could have ostensibly stopped this carnage.

When we got close to bankruptcy, I rode back in on my white charger. With the help of a tremendously dedicated team of people, we were able to fix things in under a year. In the process, I had to fire my entire senior management group, and promote a number of younger people, who rose to the occasion. It not only turned the company around, it made us a really strong operating group. With a dedicated talented team, there are no limits to what can be accomplished.

When I came back in and took over the company there were three things I had to do. The first was to get people to believe we were still in business. The second was to get music back in the stores again. The third was to get our focus back on our core business: retail music.

It took a little doing, but it came together. We still had all of our stores in great mall locations and we had our good people. The basics of the company were still in place. As soon as our people believed that we were going to be okay, we were okay. They made it happen. They turned perception into reality. All we had to do was act like the company we used to be.

Taken from a long view, what does all this mean? What lessons can be learned? First of all, don't hire consultants as employees! Secondly, if you ignore this advice and you do hire consultants, don't let them manage your company. And finally, it is a fact that sometimes, smart people do really dumb things. We violated my basic tenet: Do what you do, do it well, and do it over and over and over. All in all, I think I should have been committed.

Chapter 27

If It Ain't Broke, Don't Fix It
Mergers, acquisitions and destructions

For an entrepreneur, the great pie in the sky is to start a company from nothing, build it up to a certain size, sell it to the highest bidder, and walk away with a pot of gold. I've realized that dream twice now, and I can tell you, it's a heady experience.

If done right, mergers and acquisitions can be a great win for all parties involved. Unfortunately, that seems to be the exception rather than the rule. All too often, when one company acquires another, the result leads to disaster if not outright destruction.

One of the abiding principles of business for me is, *if it ain't broke, don't fix it*. The assumption that most companies make when acquiring another company is that the object of their acquisition is a good solid, healthy business enterprise. There is the occasional bottom fisher that goes out looking for distressed companies and tries to fix them. But most of the time, a company buys another company because it's a synergistic opportunity.

The objective is to create one very strong company out of two lesser companies while saving expenses between the two companies. Looked at on paper, this sounds like a very good idea. However many times, the corporate cultures are so different, or the egos of the acquiring company are so large that what occurs is utter chaos, and too often the acquired company is ruined in the process. The word synergy is almost a profanity in deals like this, when the acquiring company marks its territory and proceeds to piss all over the company they acquire.

The situation is often exacerbated by overly ambitious financial goals. When the goal is only money, one can expect a rough time ahead. The pressure to wring expense savings out of the merged entities too quickly leads to bad decisions. They fire good people, cut costs to a bare minimum, and break what was not broken.

Let me tell you what happened to Record Bar. In 1989, we were cranking. We had 180 stores and a plan to expand to 300 within a few years. We had established ourselves as one of the premier record store chains in the United States. The business climate in the record industry was great and we were growing like gangbusters. We weren't actively looking to sell, but people were looking to buy. We found ourselves the object of an exciting bidding war. Sometimes an opportunity presents itself when least expected. It's important to be open to whatever shows up.

The first interested party was WHSmith, the bookseller and stationer enterprise based in England. They were, and are, a fine company, nice folks. They flew my wife Arlene and me over to England, where they wined and dined us. I was very impressed with the company, their top personnel and their management philosophies. After a week of visiting with them, I changed my life goal. I wanted to become Sir Barrie!

I really wanted WHSmith to buy Record Bar. Unfortunately for us, they were savvy business investors, and they were not willing to bid above a level that made good business sense—unlike our second suitor. The company who won the bidding war was named Superclub, a Belgian company. We later came to call them Stupid Club. They gave us more money than any of us ever expected the company was worth, to the point that I never thought the deal would close. I couldn't believe anybody would pay that much, but damned if they didn't.

Superclub was in the video rental business in Belgium and Holland. They were actually a smaller company than we were, with only 40-50 stores, but they were backed with money from Philips of Holland. They were bent on worldwide domination of the audio and video retail business and they intended to get there by way of mergers and acquisitions.

To jump from a fairly small business in Europe to the big ball game in the United States was probably too lofty a goal. But these guys didn't know what they didn't know. The people who worked for Superclub in Europe were really nice folks, well meaning, earnest, if a little naïve. Unfortunately, the people they hired in the United States were some of the most incompetent business people that I ever met.

They brought in a CEO who said he didn't believe in interpersonal management. I'm not sure what other kind of management there is, but apparently he believed in managing numbers not people. He actually called people "units!"

Decisions were made that turned everything we had built into shreds. Record Bar was merged into another of Superclub's U.S. acquisitions—a far inferior company located in Atlanta. As a result, Record Bar's headquarters and corporate distribution in Durham, NC were moved to Atlanta. With that decision, they ran off a group of top-level executives it had taken me 25 years to assemble. They closed down profitable stores we had located in high-traffic malls apparently because they didn't like the mall concept. They changed our store names and destroyed priceless relationships we had built with our suppliers. If these guys were made of dynamite, they couldn't have blown their noses.

Record Bar had a bright future prior to the acquisition and merger fiasco. The Superclub purchase obliterated that future. It killed me to watch the people that had become my family be devalued, demoralized and dismissed. It was excruciatingly painful to watch something I had so lovingly built being systematically destroyed for reasons I cannot begin to fathom.

If it ain't broke, don't fix it. Acquiring companies have the right to do anything they want with their acquisition. They paid the big bucks. It's their toy. However, I will never understand why you would pay a lot of money for a toy and then break it.

Chapter 28

The Big Picture Theory
Taking a smaller piece of a bigger pie

Most people aren't cut out to be entrepreneurs. It's not that it's an exclusive club—anybody who makes the commitment can do it. It's just that it's an art. The hardest thing about the art of entrepreneurship is being able to sleep at night. If you can't be relaxed about carrying the weight of an entire enterprise on your shoulders, I am convinced that you shouldn't be an entrepreneur.

In my opinion, only about one-half-of-one-percent of the population should be entrepreneurs. While it looks great and glamorous from the outside to be your own boss, the reality is that, there is tremendous responsibility and risk. It's damn hard work. I think most people would be better off just working for somebody else.

Many people are seduced by the idea that, "I can make my own hours!" In reality you become virtually a slave to your business. If it's a retail store—you've got to be there to open the doors, and you've got to be there to close the doors, or at least make sure that somebody is there to do it. At first there is not enough money to put someone else in charge, and all the responsibility sits squarely on your shoulders.

If you are the type who is consumed by the fear of failure, you'll be running scared in a multitude of ways as an entrepreneur, and you won't be able to think clearly enough to be effective. I always had a feeling that everything was going to be okay, and for me it was. Either I was too stupid, too insensitive or too dense to understand reality—or there is something about me, and a lot of really successful entrepreneurs, that's different from most folks.

Entrepreneurship is about risk evaluation. It's about understanding just how far to push the envelope without pushing you and your organization over the edge. That is a very tricky game. Any of us who have ever played that game have at one time or another pushed too far. However if you don't push far enough, you never achieve anything worthwhile.

If you want to be an entrepreneur, it's not enough to have one location as a retailer because you'll never make enough money to make it worth the effort. It's only worth doing if you are going to expand on your idea. You not only need to have a good idea, you need to have a vision to manage and lead the people you hire to grow your enterprise larger—and the stomach for risk to grow it even more.

The hardest decision that any sole proprietorship or family enterprise makes is to add employees, open a second location, or place the first cash register outside of the family control. The first time you have to face a business situation when you aren't there to do it personally requires a great deal of trust and the ability to relinquish control. It's the only choice you have if you intend to expand. Expanding necessitates that you step back from the details so that you have the time and resources to manage the bigger picture, determining the direction and developing a strategy to get there.

As our company grew, I developed my Big Picture Theory: "It's better to take a smaller piece of a bigger pie." As you expand, you'll get a smaller and smaller piece of the overall pie in terms of percentage, but as the pie keeps expanding and you keep getting a slice, your gross dollars increase. The more you grow while maintaining profits, the more potential you have for financial gain.

If you want to get rich as an entrepreneur, you must be willing to grow and expand way beyond what you can personally control. That's just the way it is. If you are not prepared to expand on your original idea, don't do it at all. Don't ever start. Go work for someone else, it's a lot easier, and you won't carry the burden of all the responsibility.

Having said that, I don't recommend becoming an entrepreneur if you're only in it for the money. It's hard work, the demands are relentless and you must be deeply dedicated to stay the course for the long run. If you are going to take on that kind of commitment, do it for the love of it, because you have a passion for the work, or because you enjoy the game.

To me entrepreneurship is the greatest of all business games because it's your game. It's your own creation. And you get to call the shots. If you've got an appetite for risk and you have what it takes to succeed, the rewards can be enormous.

Epilogue:

Work is Vastly Overrated

The purpose of this book is to be the antidote to all the stupid stuff out there that passes for business conduct, to show from the trenches that you don't have to be a jerk when the pressure's on, that it is indeed possible to build a business and still sleep at night.

Now that I am mostly retired I can say with certainty that work is vastly overrated. It sounds like a smart-ass thing to say and, coming from somebody who has been successful enough not to have to work anymore, it's probably not the most modest thing to say either. But the more I think about what it really means to me, the more I think there is truth in this statement.

I've gotten very tired of hearing people espouse their megalomaniacal-driven business theories. I don't believe you have to be a jerk to be successful in business. I don't believe that you have to treat people like dirt to be successful either. I believe you can be a nice guy (or a nice woman) and be very successful in business—and in life. It has worked for me. I've always approached business with the attitude that if it's not going to be fun, why do it?

Too many of us become our work. We derive all of our status and all of our ego gratification from what we do for a living. There has to be meaning in our lives other than what we do for our gainful employment. Our society places special emphasis on what we do in our jobs. Even though you volunteer at a homeless shelter on Saturdays and help build houses for Habitat for Humanity on Sundays, you get little respect from an achievement-oriented society if you work at a fast food place during the week. It seems to me that one's overall contribution to society is a better way to measure individual value.

I think we should have play training in school. Too many miss out on the joys of living a balanced life. It's incredible to me that we start assigning status early in life by where a child goes to nursery school.

The big winner of course is attending an Ivy League college, with a few Dukes and Stanfords thrown in. Going to one of these schools is a ticket to great wealth and fame in the business world. Although this is a gross exaggeration, there is a pervasive belief in our society that it's true. If our child doesn't get into the right kindergarten to be on the fast track to business success, we feel we have somehow failed them. We spend so much of our early training getting ready to work, but we don't spend any time getting ready for not working.

When we sold Record Bar, I worried for months before the closing about all the stories I'd heard about people retiring early, only to die soon after. I was 47 years old and I sure as hell didn't want to whither away and die from lack of stimulation. I launched a couple of small businesses, I opened an office, and I kept my personal assistant with me, all in hopes of feeling gainfully employed. I felt bad about not getting a paycheck, even though I had become financially independent.

It took me a few years of going to an office everyday to realize that I didn't want to go to an office everyday — that I didn't *need* to go to an office everyday. We all have a drive to quit. That's what we are all working for, so we can quit someday. But when we quit we don't know what to do with ourselves. So here's my parting gift to you, a primer on learning how to play again.

The first thing you have to do is learn how to just sit there and do nothing. Spend time just being. Learn how to do that and be okay with it. You can start with five minutes a day and work up to longer periods of time, in a few months you can maybe do an hour.

Then take a walk on the wild side and go sit by the ocean, I mean let's get a little crazy! Go take a hike in the mountains, just to experience something that is fun and bigger than yourself with no particular outcome other than to just do it.

I'll bet you if you could get people to tell you the truth, they'd tell you that 95% of peak experiences have nothing to do with work. It's all about other stuff. It certainly is for me. Watching my daughters being born, just being with my wife enjoying each other's company, watching a killer sunset, sitting in St. Barths having a piña colada—those are the best experiences. When I try to think back on peak business triumphs—I can't think of any, other than selling the company. I can't remember anytime when I went to work and said, "Damn this is fabulous!" I mean I always enjoyed work, and I had a lot of fun, but it didn't rise to the level of a true peak experience.

Working is vastly overrated; we put too much value on it. Play is undervalued. Too often we work our butts off until we can't work any more due to health issues or total burnout, and then we don't have the resources to enjoy the time off.

Our life expectancy is longer these days and retirement age is getting older. Don't wait for retirement to start having those peak experiences. Get yourself a book of fun tickets and go out and get them punched!

Acknowledgements

Thanks to Lauren Sullivan, without whom the book would never have been written. Thanks to my family, Kim, Steve, Janis, Jeff, Jake, and Julia for their love and support. Thanks to Josh and Babs for their guidance and understanding, while I endlessly told stories. Thanks to Dick and Jenny for providing the wine that helped me find truth and to Eddie and Bobbie for getting us to Santa Barbara. Thanks to Meghan for keeping me thin and to Adela for making me fat. Thanks to Kathy Mills for arranging our lives, to Vickie Sullivan for helping me find my voice, to Pat Lobrutto for being an ace editor, and to Milton Kahn for helping the world find this book. Thanks to all of the people I've worked with over the years who helped me gain the insights, that are recorded in this book. And thanks again to Arlene. I would never have finished the book, if she hadn't threatened me with bodily harm. Also thanks to Justin Straus for teaching me perseverance.

Made in the USA